ACKNOWLEDGEMENTS

Sincere thanks are due to the many individuals who provided in
this book during my research into the pleasure boats at Brid
Holland, who's knowledge and advice were invaluable, Sarah _____ and the staff at
Bridlington Local Studies Library who gave immeasurable help and assistance with the
records in the Bridlington Room, archivist Ruth McDonald, the Bridlington Harbour
Commissioners and the Lord Feoffees who gave access to the Harbour records at the Bayle
Museum, Mike Wilson whose book Any More for Sailing? gave me the incentive to
research the pleasure boats, Peter Richardson and Roy Simpson owners of the Yorkshire
Belle, Bob Pickering owner of the powerboats Purla and Sonic, Arthur Newby who gave
advice and access to his photographs, Mike Milner who provided new information on *Boys'
Own* and Peter Chapman who obtained the names of the wartime crew of the *Yorkshire Belle*
from the Commonwealth War Graves Commission. Thanks are also due to Scarborough
Library, Hull Maritime Museum, The National Maritime Museum and Bridlington Harbour
Heritage Museum. Some images are from photographs taken by the author and from old
postcards in the authors collection. Where appropriate every effort has been made to trace
the copyright owner and for images referenced authors photograph and authors drawing
the copyright belongs with the author. All images are credited with their source where
known and if any image is wrongly credited then I apologise.

BIBLIOGRAPHY

The Annals of Bridlington (1867 – 1942) indexed news cuttings in Bridlington Library
The Bridlington Free Press and Chronicle newspapers– various articles and reports
Any More for Sailing? by Mike Wilson.
Cook, Welton & Gemmell 1883 – 1963 by Michael Thompson.
Pleasure Steamers of Old Yorkshire by Arthur Godfrey.
Passenger Steamers of the River Fal and Steamers and Ferries of Cornwall by Alan
Kittridge
United Towing 1920 – 1990 by Alan Ford.

Front Cover: The *Yorkshire Belle* approaching Bridlington Harbour in May 2007
(Authors photograph)
Back Cover: The crew of the Boy's Own in 1938/39. Back row from left, Walter Newby,
Barman – unidentified, Accordionist – unidentified. Middle row from left, Frank Johnson,
John Newby, George Johnson, James Newby (Snr.). Front row with lifebelt, James Newby
(Jnr.) (Harbour Heritage Museum)

First published 2010
© Frank Bull 2010
(Author)

ISBN 978-1-4457-2541-3

Contents

The Paddle steamers

The Screw Driven Pleasure Boats

The Smaller Pleasure Boats

BRIDLINGTON PLEASURE BOATS
From Paddle Steamers to Theme Boats

Paddle Steamer *Frenchman* in Bridlington Harbour about 1910

By Frank Bull

1
The Scarborough Connection

The Paddle steamers *Transit, Confidence, Friends,*
Forth, Cambria and *Scarborough*

Paddle steamers operated up and down the East Coast as early as the 1820's but it was the 1850's before the pleasure boat trade along the Yorkshire coast really took off. This trade was primarily centered on Scarborough due to its popularity as a holiday resort and its convenient location midway between the two other holiday resort towns of Whitby and Bridlington. The leading exponent was Jeremiah Hudson whose first paddle steamer, the sloop rigged paddle tug *Transit*, was brought to Scarborough in April 1852 and became the first steamboat to be registered and owned there. *Transit* was built of wood at Shields in 1848 for Leith and was 65.6 feet (20m) long and weighed 14 tons. From 1852 she ran daily pleasure trips in the summer season between Scarborough, Bridlington and other east coast ports. Visitors paid 3 shillings (15p) for the return trip between Scarborough and Bridlington. *Transit* did not actually enter Bridlington harbour so passengers who wished to land had to pay an additional fee to the local cobles to take them ashore and take them back to the *Transit*. In 1854 after only two seasons *Transit* was sold and re-registered at Sunderland, her replacement was the much larger 80 ton, iron built steamer *Éclat* of 1854. Over the next few years Jeremiah Hudson owned various other vessels including the *Fame* of 1857 and *Contraste* of 1882.

By the late 1850's paddle steamers had become commonplace along the Yorkshire coast during the summer months, much to the dismay of the local coble owners who regarded the 'summer pleasuring' or 'spawing' as their preserve. They also lost out when the paddle steamers were used to ferry passengers out to the *General Havelock* which sailed between Sunderland and London, calling at Scarborough each way. The 1868 *General Havelock* was a 670 ton passenger and cargo steamship with a single iron screw; she was wrecked in 1894 but quickly replaced by a second *General Havelock steamship*. The return fare from Scarborough to London in the late 1890's being twelve shillings (60p) in the fore cabin and eighteen shillings (90p) in the saloon, equal to £35 and £52 today. The Sunderland-Scarborough–London service ran until the start of WW 1 in 1914.

Between 1852 and 1900 Scarborough operators had built up a large fleet of paddle steamers, so many in fact, that a contemporary report stated that the harbour was *"chock-a-block"* with them. Some of these steamers operated primarily as standby tugs and others as paddle trawlers. During the summer season they were used for pleasure trips. During this innovative period Bridlington fisherman showed little interest in paddle trawlers or in developing a 'home based' pleasure boat trade.

With the coming of the railways and development of Bridlington as a holiday resort, the pleasure boat trade at Bridlington harbour relied solely upon the large number of paddle steamers operating from Scarborough and although any of them could have visited Bridlington the three known and recorded as doing so were *Transit, Confidence and Friends*.

Confidence, a 103 ton paddle steamer owned by the Royal Mail Steamboat Co. was built in 1862 at Jacksons Yard Middlesbrough. She was used to carry passengers between Middlesbrough, Whitby and Scarborough and in her first year carried the politician and future Prime Minister W. E. Gladstone and his entourage when he visited Middlesbrough. In August 1863 she came to Scarborough and made daily trips to Whitby and Bridlington. In the winter she was used for the less glamorous task of towing colliers on the river Tees.

The *Friends* of 1866, a 75 ton paddle tug built in Shields and captained by George Legg was a regular visitor to Bridlington from 1866 onwards. Although best remembered as a pleasure boat, *Friends* was actually a salvage and towing tug and it was only during the summer months that she carried passengers between the East Coast ports.

(Bridlington Library)

Paddle Steamer *Friends* in Bridlington Harbour

Friends was working out of Bridlington for the summer season in 1874 when she broke a con-rod while off Speeton Cliffs. A small boat was launched to seek help at Flamborough but before it reached there the Admiralty yacht *HMS Enchantress* came into view. After some discussion between the Lords of the Admiralty on board the yacht, *Friends* was towed into the safety of Bridlington Bay.

The overloading of pleasure boats was common as can be seen in many period photographs that show them packed with smiling holiday makers. In 1871 police checks on passengers disembarking from the paddle tug *Victor'* at Scarborough counted a total of 373 people; the vessel was only licensed for 190! The master was subsequently fined five shillings and one penny (about 26p) for each excess passenger, making a total of £71 18s 6p which would be equal to about £3,200 today.

After 1866 the most regular and best known visitor to Bridlington was the paddle steamer *Scarborough*. Built by Messrs Lewis and Co. in London in 1866 for the Gainsborough United Steam Packet Co. Ltd, she weighed 142 tons, was 150 feet (45.75m) long and described as one of the fastest and best finished paddle steamers afloat; she made the journey from London to Scarborough in 22 hours. On her arrival in the summer of 1866 the Grimsby registered *Scarborough* was the largest paddle steamer to be based at Scarborough and dominated the pleasure steamer scene for the next forty eight years.

In 1884 she was running excursions from Scarborough to Whitby and Bridlington on alternate days and had a narrow escape in September of that year when, proceeding to Bridlington with over 200 passengers on board, she was caught in a dense fog.

Paddle Steamer *Scarborough* at Scarborough

Proceeding at slow speed she suddenly found that she was running right upon Flamborough Head, the distance being a little over twenty yards (18.3m). *Scarborough* stopped within a very few yards of the rock, backed off and arrived at Bridlington only two hours behind time. The incident caused some alarm at the time, several of the passengers fainting, while others began making preparations to save themselves in case the vessel ran on the rocks. *Scarborough* did not make the return journey that night, and the passengers were compelled to return to Scarborough by train.

Not all paddle steamers had Scarborough as their home port, although it featured a great deal in their itineraries. The 1871 Tyne built *Emu* was from Whitby and the 1883 Shields built *Forth* was from Grangemouth, both were running pleasure trips to East Coast resorts in this period. *Emu* a 73 ton paddle tug owned by G. Wraith suffered the indignity of running aground in full view of holidaymakers at Scarborough Spa in 1888 - a fairly detailed penknife 'sketch' of her is carved on a pew in Whitby Parish Church. *Forth,* a 144 ton paddle steamer also ran onto the beach at Scarborough's South Bay in 1899.

In 1899 the Harbour Commissioners at Scarborough purchased the 1879 Preston built 174 ton iron paddle tug *Cambria* for £850 to use as both a tug and pleasure boat. Although *Cambria* in her current state would require a lot of work to make her suitable for both tasks, the Commissioners knew this and had bought the vessel cheaply. After nine months in a Sunderland dock and the expenditure of £1650 *Cambria* was ready for service and was to prove popular both as a pleasure-boat and as a paddle tug.

Paddle Steamer *Cambria* at Scarborough in the early 1900's

2
Bridlington's Own Paddle Steamer

The Arrival of the Paddle Tug *Frenchman*

In July 1899 Bridlington gained its own harbour based paddle steamer with the arrival of the 119 ton steel paddle tug *Frenchman*. Built as the *Coquet* for H. Andrews of Newcastle in 1892 at South Shields by J. P. Rennoldson & Son, she was 90.3 feet (27.6m) in length with a beam of 19.2 feet (5.8m) and she had two side level surface condensing engines driving her large paddle wheels. The single cylinder engines, which were also built by J. P. Rennoldson & Son, had a bore / stroke of 25 x 45 inches (63.5 x 114.3cm) and operated at 45 lbs (3.1 bars) pressure. They were capable of providing 225 indicated horse power and gave her a service speed of 10.5 knots.

Coquet was sold by her Newcastle owners in 1899 to T. Gray and Co., put on the Hull register and renamed *Frenchman*. Designed for towing and salvage work, she was employed as a paddle tug on the Humber and was adapted by her builders for excursion work in the summer months, returning to towage duties during the winter months. In good weather her top deck was open to the elements but she could unfurl a tarpaulin cover over a framework on her aft deck when it rained.

(Authors Collection)

Paddle Tug *Frenchman* in Bridlington Bay in the early 1900's

Frenchman would become a firm favorite with the Bridlington holiday makers and got off to a flying start in 1899 by making frequent trips in the bay, between her first appearances in July to her departure in September she had made over 110 pleasure trips, seventeen of them in a single day on the 14th August. *Frenchman* and *Scarborough* could often be seen together in Bridlington where they dominated the harbour and, with a capacity of 246 and 300 passengers respectively, they dominated the local pleasure trade as well. Together they provided a summer season of pleasure trips for East Coast holidaymakers. *Frenchman* usually arrived at Bridlington in May in time for the Whitsuntide holiday, running short trips in the bay and longer trips to other local resorts, being based at Bridlington until the end of the season in September. *Scarborough* had a similar summer season at Scarborough, Whitsuntide to September, but a different itinerary, she ran trips from Scarborough to Bridlington with holidaymakers spending time ashore until she left on her return trip to Scarborough, occasionally she ran trips in the bay while at Bridlington but did not stay overnight unless weather or engine trouble forced cancellation of her return trip.

Their domination of the local pleasure trade did not stop the occasional visits by other paddle steamers and both *Forth* and *Cambria* made several visits to Bridlington in the early 1900's. The Grangemouth registered *Forth* is known to have made several visits to Bridlington in 1900, although like *Cambria* these visits were not made on a regular full time basis. In 1900 *Forth* was also given the contract for ferrying Scarborough passengers out to the coastal steamer *General Havelock*. *Cambria* when working as a pleasure boat ran pleasure trips to places of interest along the coast including several visits to Bridlington from 1900 until 1913 and as a tug she refloated the 580 ton Norwegian steamer *Bjorn* in June 1900. In December she rescued the crew of the stranded steamer *San Antonio*. In 1912 *Cambria* herself ran aground near Gristhorpe, although no-one was seriously hurt the passengers were badly shaken. *Cambria* was refloated and sold to Hull owners in 1913, Scarborough Harbour Commissioners then ceased to own any paddle-boats and *Cambria's* history after 1913 is not recorded.

Though pleasure cruising is inherently safe, *Frenchman* was involved in a most unfortunate incident in August 1905. The Bridlington Free Press reported the death of a crew member who was lost overboard during a pleasure trip around Flamborough Head. Despite a holidaymaker from Dublin diving in to save him, the 22-year-old ship's steward, George Hodgson, of Hull, vanished beneath the waves off the King and Queen Rocks. He had been acting as a collector of fares and it was thought at the time he fell in he would have had his pockets weighed down with seven or eight pounds worth of silver and other coins, which may have dragged him underwater. His body was later washed ashore at Flamborough. An inquest was held on September the 23rd 1905 which revealed that the steward could not swim and that he had been collecting water in a bucket to which he had attached a rope and thrown it into the sea from a position on the rear of a paddle sponson and outside of the protecting stanchions and guard chains. The second engineer stated that the steward should not have been in this unprotected position; other witnesses stated that they thought the force of water in the bucket had pulled him over. After hearing all the evidence the Jury returned a verdict of accidental death and donated their jury shillings to the widow's fund for which Captain Spence thanked them and said the fund currently amounted to £72. Part of the money had been raised by *Frenchman* doing a special benefit trip in aid of the fund.

This tragic incident did not diminish *Frenchman's* popularity and when she returned to Bridlington in June 1906 she had been lengthened at the stern by 10.1 feet (3m), reportedly to increase passenger capacity. Her gross tonnage increased to 137 tons and her draft decreased from 9.4 feet to 9.3 feet (2.8m). After lengthening her No. 4 certificate entitled her to carry 246 passengers on trips out of Bridlington Harbour.

(Bridlington Library)

Paddle tug *Frenchman* in Bridlington Harbour c1908

Although *Frenchman* was only based in Bridlington during the summer months, this did not exclude an occasional 'out of season' visit, one of which occurred on the 8th November 1910 when she arrived in the harbour in company with her screw driven sister tugs *Kinsman* (built 1908) and *Handyman* (built 1909). The reason for this visit by three tugs from T Gray and Company is not given but it provided harbour dues of 13 shillings (65p – but about £34 in today's money) at a slack time of the year. By 1913 *Frenchman* was making daily trips to sea at sixpence (2½p) to Flamborough Head and Speeton Cliffs, one shilling (5p) to Hornsea and one shilling to Scarborough. In comparison *Scarborough's* passengers could reserve seats on the bridge deck for the princely sum of five shillings (25p). It had also become traditional for pleasure boats to carry musicians to entertain the passengers and *Scarborough* could boast three such entertainers, the other paddle steamers followed suit but in some instances their 'band' consisted of a single musician.

In 1914 *Frenchman* arrived as usual on 6th June, followed by *Scarborough* on the 2nd July. The summer season had only just started when on Tuesday morning 21st July 1914 *Scarborough* was involved in a similar 'fog' incident to the one 30 years earlier. Leaving Scarborough harbour with about 200 passengers for a return trip to Bridlington, *Scarborough* ran into a dense fog off Filey Brig. Captain Kimmings allowed the vessel to proceed slowly and with utmost caution, the fog lifted slightly and he arrived at Bridlington about half an hour later than usual. At about 2.30 *Frenchman* left the harbour for a cruise to Speeton cliffs with *Scarborough* following on her return journey to Scarborough at 2.45 p.m., both steamers ran into a wall of fog off Flamborough Head, *Frenchman* turned around and went for a cruise off Barmston while *Scarborough* waited to see if the fog lifted. However the fog became so thick that the bows of the ship could not be seen from the bridge, the Flamborough fog horn was booming from the cliff top and vessels nearby were sounding their fog horns. Captain Kimmings decided to return to Bridlington and arrived back in the harbour at 4.45 p.m., passengers were informed that they could return with the ship when the weather cleared or return by rail and make a return journey another day at the single fare price. The captains concern for the passengers comfort was much appreciated and he was given three cheers on the pier at Bridlington for his refusal to take any risks. In the evening about 8 o'clock the weather cleared and *Scarborough* left on her return journey, there were few passengers most having returned by train or were staying the night in Bridlington. These two incidents illustrate not only the vagaries of the east coast weather but also the calm and professional way both experienced captains handled the situation.

On the 4th August 1914 Britain's declaration of war with Germany did little to dampen the pleasure trade, everyone assuming that it "would be over by Christmas", by the 21st August the North Eastern Railway Company had removed railway restrictions and re-commenced cheap excursion fares to Bridlington, with cheap weekend tickets to continue until further notice. On August 28th excursion trains brought hundreds of people from Hull, Leeds and Sheffield to Bridlington. *Scarborough* made a visit to Bridlington on the very day that war was declared, following this with two more visits in August and two more in September. However it would not be over by Christmas and unbeknown to the people watching the departure of *Scarborough* on the 3rd September 1914 at the end of her season, it would be the last time she would be seen at Bridlington. After her return to Scarborough the 48 year old paddle steamer quietly sailed away to the breakers yard to be scrapped.

Eleven days later on the 14th September, *Frenchman,* by now chartered by the military and naval authorities for defence duties, also departed Bridlington and there would be no more pleasure steamers for nearly five long weary years.

After the war, *Frenchman* was quickly overhauled and repainted. In May 1919 the Bridlington Chronicle proudly announced that *Frenchman* would be stationed in Bridlington for the summer season and subsequently confirmed her arrival date as June 7th.

The Whitsuntide holiday crowds were delighted to see the familiar shape of *Frenchman* entering Bridlington harbour under the command of her popular and regular Captain, George Spence, to take up her pleasure boat duties once again. With *Scarborough* gone *Frenchman* had the pleasure steamer trade to herself.

Frenchman quickly adapted to her postwar itinerary of providing pleasure trips for Bridlington holidaymakers during the summer season and each year her arrival would be announced beforehand in the local press. She usually left Minerva pier, Hull, about midday on the Saturday before Whit-Monday, running down the Humber with holiday makers on board, round Spurn Point and along the coast to Bridlington, the whole trip taking some six hours. Her arrival would be greeted by large numbers of spectators lining the piers to welcome her back. Her pleasure trips were very similar to those made pre-war - frequent trips in the bay, round the headland, Speeton and Bempton cliffs and occasional trips to Hornsea and Scarborough. At the end of the season in September, her departure would be watched by equally large crowds, with streamers being thrown and farewell blasts on the ships whistle. Her Captain, George Spence, was one of her longest-serving captains and there were frequent remarks about his good seamanship. In September 1921, with rough seas in Bridlington bay it was reported that

> *"The Frenchman made harbour. It rolled a good deal but Captain Spence had no difficulty negotiating the harbour entrance. The passengers seemed to thoroughly enjoy the rolling of the ship as it came in."*

Slack trade and fierce competition led to a rationalization of the Humber towing business and in 1921 a merger of the interests of T. Gray and Co., owners of the *Frenchman,* along with several other local towing companies resulted in the formation of The United Towing Co. Ltd. The new ownership however did not change the use of *Frenchman* as a pleasure paddle tug in the summer season and she carried on as before with yearly visits to Bridlington.

In June 1922 two hundred passengers were on board for Frenchman's return to Bridlington from Hull for the summer season. Coming round the Spurn and heading north for Bridlington, a headwind

> *"Made the ship somewhat lively and a few passengers suffered from mal-de-mer".*

In 1925 many people were saddened to read of the sudden death of Captain George Spence, the popular skipper of *Frenchman* had died suddenly on April 1st, after a seizure. He was only 63 years old. With *Frenchman* going from strength to strength at Bridlington, a replacement paddle steamer was badly needed at Scarborough and the situation was finally rectified in 1925 when the *Bilsdale* arrived to carry on the paddle steamer tradition at that port.

3
The Last Paddle Steamers

Frenchman and *Bilsdale* the last of the Yorkshire Pleasure Paddle steamers

(Bridlington Library)

Paddle Steamer *Bilsdale* about to enter Bridlington harbour

Bilsdale was originally built as the paddle steamer *Lord Roberts* at Preston in 1900 by W. Allsup & Sons for the Great Yarmouth Steam Tug Co. Ltd., *Lord Roberts* was some 200 feet (61m) long with a displacement of 199 tons and powered by a non-compound double diagonal engine. Originally she had an open bridge but a covered wheelhouse and other improvements were added later and her displacement increased to 235 tons. As *Lord Roberts* she had sailed from Yarmouth to Lowestoft on excursion work and was capable of carrying 386 passengers. In 1911 and 1912 she was chartered by Cosens & Company to run out of Weymouth in place of *Empress*, which was working out of Swanage with *Monarch*. The *Lord Roberts* was requisitioned in 1914 for war service as the *Earl Roberts* and on decommissioning in 1919 she was sold to the Furness Shipbuilding Company for use at their shipyard. *Earl Roberts / Lord Roberts* was sold again in 1925 to the Crosthwaite Steamship Company of Middlesbrough who renamed her *Bilsdale* and based her at Scarborough for the summer holiday season

    Although popular with the holidaymakers, *Bilsdale* never seemed to achieve the local affection enjoyed by *Scarborough*. One reason may be that unlike her predecessor she was not a 'Scarborough' boat - she was owned, registered and crewed in Middlesbrough and came to Scarborough each year just for the holiday season. Commanded by Captain C. W. Duncan, *Bilsdale* took holidaymakers on pleasure trips from Scarborough but surprisingly apart from the photograph showing *Bilsdale* about to enter Bridlington harbour there is little other evidence, photographic or written, to indicate how often she came to Bridlington and It is unclear if she was a regular caller like *Scarborough* or an occasional visitor like *Cambria* and *Forth*. The Crosthwaite Steamship Company may have been content to leave the Bridlington pleasure boat trade to their main rival *Frenchman* which continued her yearly pleasure trips from Bridlington until Wednesday September 28th 1927 when, under the command of Captain Dalgleish, she left for the Humber after what proved to be her final season. On board were some twenty five passengers for Hull and a large crowd on the pier to bid them goodbye. Streamers were thrown and as she left the quay the two banjoists on board struck up 'Auld Lung Syne'. Her departure was watched with even greater interest than usual, for she was towing the motor launch *Babs* to Hull to be re-fitted, *Frenchman* and her charge steamed off and were soon lost from sight in the morning haze. About an hour later a loud blast on the hooter was heard and *Frenchman* was seen returning, a strong southerly wind had made it impossible to safely tow *Babs* to Hull. The motor-coble *Kathleen* took over the tow and brought *Babs* back into the harbour, allowing *Frenchman* to continue its journey.

Frenchman had been based at Bridlington for every summer season from 1899 to 1914 and then from 1919 to 1927 a grand total of 24 years. During this period she had safely carried hundreds of thousands of holiday visitors and residents on pleasure trips in the bay, along the coast and visited numerous local resorts. She had carried out various towing tasks on the Humber and had 'done her bit in the war'.

Bilsdale now had the paddle steamer pleasure trade to herself but her popularity within the local Scarborough fishing community had not improved, the local fishermen offering trips round the bay in their much smaller boats resented this 'outsider' pushing in to cream off 'their' business. This animosity boiled over late on the night of Monday 27 August 1928 when there was a 'punch-up' on the pier involving two local fishermen and some *Bilsdale* crewmen that culminated in *Bilsdale* deckhand Frederick Thompson of Middlesbrough, being knocked into the harbour. Thompson should have suffered no more than a ducking but he had the ill-luck to fall heavily on to a small platform on the *Bilsdale's* hull before dropping into the water and sinking. The two Scarborough men and Thompson's mates went to his rescue but it was some time before he was found and hauled out, dying in hospital a few hours later. The two Scarborough men were charged with murder but when the local magistrates heard the case they reduced the charge to manslaughter and sent the two men for trial at York Assizes. They were found guilty but the judge was quite impressed with them, referring to "their very decent characters", and took the view that a number of the men in the punch-up were "in drink". The fishermen, who had spent five weeks in the cells while on remand, ended up being bound over for three years to keep the peace - plus a lecture from the judge about keeping off the drink in future.

Although 1927 was the last year of operation as a pleasure boat at Bridlington for *Frenchman*, she still had some useful life left and had spent 1928 working on the Humber and making short pleasure trips in addition to any towing duties. On February 21st 1929 under the command of Captain Sizer she made a surprise return to Bridlington but not as a pleasure boat. *Frenchman* was under charter to the Air Ministry to tow out the buoys to mark the area of the new RAF bombing range at Skipsea. In the afternoon she took Air Ministry official Captain Greenwood and others out to conduct a survey of the range area. She then returned to working on the Humber but later in 1929 the LNER Company started running their ferries as excursion boats at half the price being charged by *Frenchman* and she was taken out of service. Later her superstructure, engines, paddle wheels etc. were removed and the hull, moored at the Church Lane wharf on the river Hull, was used by United Towing as a dumb barge for coaling other vessels. An inglorious end for the paddle steamer which a 1920's Bridlington report described as *"one of this pleasure resort's greatest assets"*.

Bilsdale continued to sail from Scarborough until 1934 when, on the 17 September, the 34 year old paddle steamer made her last cruise out of Scarborough and was then sold for breaking up. The last pleasure paddle steamer on the Yorkshire coast had gone!

Frenchman continued to be used as a dumb barge for many years and in the early 1960's she could still be seen just below the original entrance to Victoria dock downstream of Clarence Flour Mill, Hull. Although widely reported as being towed to New Holland for scrap in 1963, F. Flintoff of Acomb York claimed to have seen a hulk, with the name *Frenchman* on the stern, still moored up as late as September 12 1965. When he returned on September 26 the hulk had gone. *Frenchman* was finally broken up at New Holland in 1968.

During the 82 years between the arrival of the paddle tug *Transit* in 1852 and the departure of the paddle steamer *Bilsdale* in 1934, various paddle steamers had visited Bridlington. The largest, by displacement, was the 235 ton *Bilsdale* but she did not 'regularly' call at Bridlington. The largest paddle steamer to have regularly called at Bridlington was the 142 ton *Scarborough* (the 174 ton Cambria and the 144 ton Forth were only occasional visitors to Bridlington). The only paddle steamer to be regularly based at Bridlington over a number of years was the 137 ton *Frenchman*. When they were withdrawn from service, *Scarborough* was 48 years old, *Frenchman* was 37 and *Bilsdale* was a relatively young 34.

Postscript

In January 2002 Dick White of Stoddy, Lancaster purchased the ships bell from *Frenchman* at an auction of maritime objects held by Bonhams. The whereabouts of the bell between *Frenchman* being taken out of service and the sale in 2002 was not recorded.

4
The Motor Boats

Girls Own, Britannia and *May Morn.*

In the mid 1800's the long standing debates on the merits of the paddle wheel versus the screw propeller were finally resolved by the well known engineer Isambard Kingdom Brunel who convinced the Royal Navy to conduct a series of trials with the screw driven steamer *Rattler*. The trials cumulated in the famous 1845 towing competitions between the *Rattler* and the paddle driven *Alecto* which proved beyond doubt the superiority of the screw. These developments had not gone unnoticed in the ship building industry and gradually the screw replaced the paddle wheel in commercial ships including pleasure steamers.

For the Bridlington pleasure steamer trade the future lay with screw driven vessels and in direct contrast to their lack of interest in the paddle steamers, Bridlington fishermen were now very keen to participate in the lucrative summer excursion trade with 'home based' pleasure boats. By working in consortiums or groups they were able to introduce their first screw driven 'pleasure boat' as early as 1922.

(L Spencer via Bridlington Library)
Girls Own entering Bridlington Harbour in the 1930's

This was the large motor boat *Girls Own* and she was the first large screw driven pleasure boat to work at Bridlington. The Chronicle for Friday April 7th 1922 reported her arrival in the harbour a few days earlier from Southend-on-Sea but who built her and exactly where was not stated. The report went on to say she was "a splendidly found craft capable of covering from 12 to 14 mph". The enterprising owners were the well known Bridlington fishermen and boatmen Jim Newby and Bride Pockley and they brought *Girls Own* to Bridlington with the intention of starting passenger trips a week later, on the eve of the Easter holiday.

Girls Own was a large wooden 'open' motor boat about 60 feet (18.3m) long, with an amidships deckhouse and open wheel station, single mast forward and her wooden hull appears to have had a natural finish. There was wooden seating along the sides for passengers but most of them are shown sitting on the deckhouse or the forecastle. The engine exhausted out of the stern via twin pipes just above the waterline, engine size or type is unrecorded. The *Girls Own* was obviously a success, for on Sunday 25th March 1923 the motor boat *Britannia* arrived from Southend-on-Sea.

(Bridlington Library)

Britannia in Bridlington Harbour c1930

Britannia was built by Hayward and Croxan (who may also have been the builders of Girls Own as they were very similar in appearance) for Richard Crawford though other reports claim she was owned by a consortium of six local fishermen. She was a 52 foot (15.8m) long wooden 'open' motor boat, with a small deckhouse and open wheel station amidships. Wooden seating was provided for passengers, a single mast fitted forward and the engine, size or type unknown, exhausted out of the stern via twin pipes in a manner similar to Girls Own. *Britannia* was usually skippered by Harry Hopper and could carry up to 100 passengers maximum, though conditions would be cramped at this and about 70 - 80 would be more reasonable. An early incident in *Britannia's* career was on July 13th 1923 when the Bridlington fishing boat *Lily of the Valley* caught fire and foundered five miles (8km) south of Flamborough Head, the crew took to a small boat and were picked up by the steam trawler *Royal Escort*. The *Royal Escort* subsequently handed the crew over to *Britannia* which brought them back to Bridlington harbour.

The two motor boats *Girls Own* and *Britannia* operated pleasure trips in the bay and were joined in 1925 by a third motor boat *May Morn* that was first seen in Bridlington harbour on May 1st 1925. She was similar in appearance to *Girls Own* and *Britannia* but possibly slightly longer as she was described as one of the largest pleasure boats in the harbour at that time. Where she came from, who built her and where is not recorded but she was owned and run by Jack Champlin who planned to run day trips during the season and whose family also owned the coble *White Heather*. *May Morn* was another 'open type' wooden boat like *Girls Own* and *Britannia* with an open wheel station at the rear of the amidships deckhouse, a single mast forward and no funnel.

Like the other two motor boats the engine, size or type unknown, exhausted out of the stern via twin pipes. Although there was wooden seating along the sides for passengers most of them seemed to prefer sitting on the deckhouse or the forecastle.

(Bridlington Library)

May Morn leaving Bridlington Harbour in the early 1930's

From 1925 *Girls Own*, *Britannia* and *May Morn* had the large motor boat trade to themselves with only the paddle tug *Frenchman* giving any realistic opposition. When *Frenchman* was withdrawn from service at the end of 1927 any thoughts of no more competition was quickly dispelled when the new twin screw steam tug - cruiser *Yorkshireman* arrived in 1928 as the replacement for the withdrawn paddle tug.

5
Competition Arrives

United Towing's Tug-Cruiser *Yorkshireman*

United Towing was forced to modernise its fleet during the 1920s following complaints that its ageing fleet lacked the power to handle large modern vessels. The company wished to continue carrying passengers in the summer months, but the *Frenchman* could not simply be replaced by sending one of their new tugs to Bridlington. Tug design had evolved since *Frenchman* was built and the latest examples had much deeper hulls to accommodate their triple expansion engines and large screw propellers. These tugs would have been severely limited in operations from Bridlington's tidal harbour and United Towing therefore commissioned Earle's Shipbuilding & Engineering Company Limited on the Humber to specifically design *Yorkshireman* as a modern replacement for *Frenchman*. *Yorkshireman* was therefore designed as a special tug-cruiser that could operate from Bridlington for summer cruising and assist stranded vessels in shallow water when used as a tug. In particular, she would be able to assist vessels that grounded on sandbanks in the Humber estuary.

(Authors Collection)

Yorkshireman at Bridlington Harbour entrance, early 1930's

Built as yard number 160104 for the United Towing Company of Hull she was a coal burning twin screw vessel of 251 gross tons, 120 feet (36.6m) long with a max. beam width of 27.1 feet (8.3m) and had a remarkable shallow draft of 7 feet 2 inches (2.3m) which allowed comfortable access to Bridlington Harbour at most times except very low water. Power was provided by two Earle's reciprocating triple expansion engines with direct acting vertical cylinders of 800 indicated horse power which gave a top speed of 11.2 knots.

    Yorkshireman had run her trials on the Humber on Thursday May 17th which her owners described as "satisfactory in every respect". They went on to say that they felt that the development of Bridlington as a seaside resort warranted a better vessel (than *Frenchman*) for passenger service and pleasure trips. *Yorkshireman* arrived in Bridlington harbour on Sunday, 26th May, 1928, and was ready for service the following day. As an excursion boat she was a two class steamer with her first class passengers having the forward and aft parts of the boat deck. The forward part of the boat deck was 'screened in' under glazed protection panels to provide cover in poor weather and as a miniature promenade deck. Second class passengers occupied the main deck and the captain had an open flying bridge above the boat deck. She also had a large lounge, a main saloon forward paneled with polished mahogany, a ladies' saloon aft and a small bar with musicians, usually comprising an accordionist and a saxophone player, providing musical entertainment in harbour and at sea. All in all *Yorkshireman's* passengers could enjoy a level of luxury they could not find on the other pleasure boats.

On the water, *Yorkshireman* looked similar to several other coal-fired tugs of her era, notably United Towing's *Norman, Krooman, Scotsman* and *Irishman*. Like those tugs, her paintwork conformed to United's colour scheme of green boot topping (a painted band just above the waterline), black topsides, white band above a rubbing strake at upper deck level, white bow plate, shelter deck plating and stanchions, white funnel with deep black top. Below decks, however, she had a flat-bottomed, shallow draught hull, with a slightly increased breadth to ensure stability. This squat hull-form lent itself to twin screw propulsion, which gave the added benefit of greater maneuverability. The engine room ventilators were painted black with white inside the cowls, other ventilators and superstructure were a warm brown colour, masts were a deep shade of brown with the main topmast painted black to mask sooting from the funnel. Awning stanchions were rigged on the bridge deck and aft over the engine room hatch and companionway and covered in hot weather. At the foremast the *Yorkshireman* usually wore a large pennant carrying her name, with her owners' house-flag at the main and though she had a gaff the Red Ensign was flown from a slender staff stepped in a semi-circular grating in the round of the stern.

Yorkshireman always went alongside starboard side to the North Pier at Bridlington so that she could put out her passenger gangway with a tall single davit fitted for the purpose on the starboard side abaft the funnel. Likewise after taking all her passengers on board, the gangway was brought aboard and she left by reversing out of the harbour mouth. After the day's work *Yorkshireman* moved across the harbour to a berth alongside the South Pier in order to coal, bags of coal were taken on board from a waiting lorry and taken below deck to the coal store. With her impressive appearance *Yorkshireman* soon became one of the best known vessels in the north east and when alongside her berth on the North Pier, her smart paintwork, white and black funnel, two tall masts, flags and bunting, her identity was beyond question. From her first arrival in 1928 she usually operated from Bridlington at Whitsuntide through to the end of the summer season in September and her arrival and departure became scenes of specific ritual. She would announce her arrival to the waiting crowds on the piers with blasts on her whistle and her departure from Bridlington was even more spectacular with maroons being fired, farewell blasts on the whistle and the musicians on board playing an appropriate farewell to the large crowds watching her leave. On 4th August 1928 to promote her first year in operation, about 100 people attended a dance on board, she left the harbour at 9pm and anchored about 500 yards from the pier where she made a very attractive sight illuminated by hundreds of small electric lamps, the strains of dance music were easily heard by people on the piers and seafront.

With the country slowly recovering from the effects of the Great War, the holiday trade began to grow larger and Bridlington again became one of the East Coasts favorite holiday destinations. *Yorkshireman* together with the motor boats *Girls Own*, *Britannia* and *May Morn* were very popular attractions and financially successful. In June 1931 *Yorkshireman* had a rare opportunity to combine her pleasure and towing duties when a young man and a woman got into difficulties in a small rowing boat owing to the choppy water. They found it impossible to row back to the harbour against the tide and realizing the seriousness of the situation the captain of *Yorkshireman* slowed up and took them on board, the rowing boat was then tied to the stern of the tug and towed into the harbour.

(Authors Collection)

Yorkshireman in Bridlington Bay

6
The halcyon Pre-War Years

The existing boats are joined by *Princess Marina, Royal Jubilee,*
New Royal Sovereign, Boys Own, Miss Mercury and Yorkshire Belle

By the early 1930's holiday makers were arriving in large numbers by excursion trains, coaches and motor cars - much to the delight of the pleasure boat operators. The railway companies in particular were keen to promote the seaside holiday excursions and produced numerous posters in the 1930's, many of which featured Bridlington as a desirable destination. For those holidaymakers wishing to cruise in the bay there was *Yorkshireman*, or "'t' steamer" as she was known, together with the large motor boats *Girls Own, May Morn* and *Britannia*.

LNER poster of the early 1930's

The Crew of the *Britannia* in the early 1930's
(left to right)
R. Crawford, E. Welburn, H. Hopper and
J. Sawdon

(Bridlington Library)

The crew of the *Britannia* during the 1930's consisted of well known Bridlington fishermen and pleasure boat men including Richard Crawford, Ernest 'Brannie' Welburn, Harry 'Tal' Hopper and James Sawdon. On June 4th 1931 members of the Ladies Lifeboat Guild boarded the pleasure boat *Britannia* and went out to meet Bridlington's new motor lifeboat the *Stanhope Smart*. In later years 'Brannie' Welburn and 'Tal' Hopper both became coxswains of the *Stanhope Smart*.

These early years were not without incident as related in the following two reports concerning *Girls Own* and *May Morn*. On Saturday 18th June 1932 *Girls Own*, with Skipper John Newby in charge, was returning from a pleasure cruise with a full complement of passengers, mostly children, when a large motor launch swung round the South Pier. With great presence of mind the skipper threw the engine into reverse gear to deaden the force of the impact. The Steel tipped bows of the motor launch tore the bow planking of the *Girls Own*, holing the vessel but well above the water line. Large numbers of people on the piers and harbour side witnessed the incident. There was no panic and the *Girls Own* was able to land her passengers safely. The motor launch was not damaged and *Girls Own* was repaired in time for business on Monday morning.

Bridlington Harbour in the late 1920's or early 1930's
Left to right, *Britannia, Girls Own* and *May Morn*

On Monday 6th August 1932 about forty visitors to Bridlington had a thrilling experience when *May Morn,* under the command of skipper R. Crawford, was forced aground by the tide and seas near the south pier, shortly after she had left the harbour. She was driven ashore broadside on in choppy water which broke over the vessel drenching the light clothes worn by most of the passengers. They however remained calm and shortly afterwards A. Hutchinson in the motor coble *Kate and Violet* went out to her with the intention of towing her off. The tide was so strong that it was found impossible to do so and there was a danger of the motor coble going aground as well. The Harbour Master, Lieutenant E. Taylor, then took over the refloating operation and two local fishermen, A. Tranmer and J. Sawdon, set off in a rowing boat to the stranded vessel. One end of a stout launch rope was fastened aboard *May Morn* and the other end was brought to the North Pier on which were a large number of holiday makers, many of them tugged so vigorously in the attempt to refloat her that the rope snapped and several of the volunteers fell in a heap. In order to lighten the vessel about half the people aboard were taken off in a ferry boat and after an exciting passage through the broken water they were safely landed at the harbour. More ropes were made fast to the *May Morn* and she was refloated by the combined efforts of the *Kate and Violet* and the people on the North Pier and proceeded into the harbour. Although she had been aground for about one and a half hours *May Morn* was undamaged, the remaining people on board, their clothes drenched by spray, did not appear to be any the worse for their experience, several of them declared that they had really enjoyed it.

Photographs of *May Morn* show that she underwent some extensive rework during the Late 1930's. The open wheel station was moved to the front of a newly added small funnel, her hull was painted white and she had two masts instead of one. The addition of the small funnel and the repositioning of the wheel station would indicate that she had probably been re-engined with the exhaust now venting into the funnel rather than through twin pipes at the stern as before.

With the ever increasing numbers of holiday makers coming to Bridlington, there was obviously room for more boats to meet the demand and in 1935 two more large pleasure boats arrived namely *Princess Marina* and *Royal Jubilee*.

Princess Marina arrived in Bridlington in March 1935 from Yarmouth where she had been purchased by Albert Butler of Leeds.

(Bridlington Library)

Princess Marina in Bridlington Bay

Princess Marina had started life in mid-March 1928 as *Brit*, built by Fellows and Co Ltd. of Yarmouth, yard number 322, official number 144157, as a coastal and river boat for owners E. W. & S. H. D. Longfield, who ran cruises along the Norfolk coast. She was powered by two Kelvin petrol-paraffin engines, which were a popular form of engine until true diesel engines were perfected, and was over 60 feet (18m) long, with a beam of 14.75 feet (4.5m). She ran cruises from Britannia Pier and Hall Quay Yarmouth and from other South Coast resorts until she was sold to Albert Butler in 1935 for operations from Bridlington. In the six weeks before she made her first voyage under her new name of *Princess Marina*, Albert Butler had numerous improvements made including the provision of a saloon. She had a rounded stern, engines and steering controlled from a small, tall covered wheelhouse amidships. There was a single funnel behind the wheelhouse, leaving large clear open areas forward and aft for passengers. The area aft of the funnel had a tubular steel framework which extended almost to the stern over which a canvas awning could be spread to provide covering for the passengers. Masts were fitted forward and aft but no separate ships boat or lifeboat was carried. On Saturday 20th April 1935, *Princess Marina*, suitably decorated with flags and creating a great deal of interest among the crowds lining the harbour, made her first voyage from Bridlington. In civic recognition of the latest addition to Bridlington's fleet of pleasure steamers, the Mayor, Cllr. J. A. Drew entered the wheelhouse and with skipper Richard Crawford at his side, steered the *Princess Marina* into the Bay for a 15-minute trip. Other civic guests on board included the Town Clerk, three Councillors and the Harbour Master.

The second large pleasure boat to arrive in 1935 was the *Royal Jubilee*. The *Royal Jubilee* had been newly built in 1935, the year of King George V's silver jubilee and was the first pleasure boat to be built by Beverley boat builders Cook, Welton & Gemmell Ltd. (CWG) who were better known as builders of steam trawlers.

(Bridlington library)

Royal Jubilee on a pleasure trip from Bridlington Harbour about 1937

Her yard number was 603, her official number was 163995 and her owners were Crawford and Pockley of Bridlington, whom it is believed were acting for a consortium of six local fishermen that also operated *Girls Own* and *Britannia*. A CWG shipyard drawing has the name *Royal Sovereign* which has been crossed out, this name may have been dropped due to the planned arrival of the *New Royal Sovereign* in 1936 and the CWG vessel renamed *Royal Jubilee* in honour of King George V's silver jubilee in the year she was built. Powered by twin Bergius built three-cylinder Kelvin K3 diesel engines developing 132 horsepower and driving twin screws *Royal Jubilee* had a gross tonnage of 60, a registered length of 69 feet 6 inches (21.2m), an overall length of 74 feet (22.5m) and a maximum beam width of 17 feet (5.2m). She could accommodate up to 200 passengers and her hull, machinery and equipment were designed to comply with Board of Trade requirements for a steam 6 passenger certificate with plying limits based on Bridlington.

As the first pleasure boat from CWG her layout was influential in subsequent designs from them and therefore it is worth describing her in greater detail.

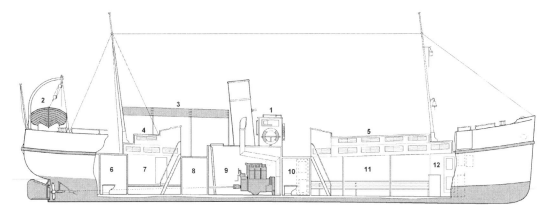

(Authors Drawing)

Section through *Royal Jubilee* showing layout

Her engines and steering were controlled from an elevated wheel station (1) on the deck; this was protected by a wrap around 4 foot (1.2m) high screen to the front and sides. Masts were fitted forward and aft and a 10 foot (3m) long ships boat (2), called an 'accident' boat, was lashed across her cruiser type stern. Steel framework (3) extended aft from the funnel to the rear mast over which a canvas awning could be spread to provide covering for the passengers. The main deck was in Borneo pine and sparred seating in teak was provided around most of the deck sides together with 'buoyant' seating at the bow and stern. Teak skylights (4) and (5) on the deck provided natural light to the saloon and lobby areas Her deep hull contained a ladies toilet (6), ladies lobby (7), store room (8), engine room (9), gents toilet (10), passenger saloon (11) and bar (12).

The ladies lobby had two wooden bench seats and was flanked on its sides by large store rooms, it was only 8 foot by 6 foot (2.4m x 1.2m) so is unlikely to have accommodated thirty as claimed in the local press on her arrival. The full width engine room held the two diesel engines side by side together with their separate 140 gallon capacity (636.4 litres) fuel tanks. The main passenger saloon was nearly 21 feet (6.4m) long and also ran across the full width of the hull. Sparred seating in teak was provided down each side and at the end by the toilet. The forward end of the saloon contained a bar that provided a counter service to passengers, small, tables were provided and the floor had a linoleum covering.

Royal Jubilee was launched in Beverley on the 4th July 1935 in the presence of her owners and local dignitaries from Bridlington. Miss L. Twidle, daughter of Mr. A. S. Twidle J. P., the managing director of CWG christened her *Royal Jubilee*. After launching, *Royal Jubilee* underwent Board of Trade tests and was approved & registered on the 18th of July 1935. On her cruises from Bridlington *Royal Jubilee* had a crew of six and was captained by J. R. Newby, the former skipper of *Girls Own*. *Royal Jubilee* was intended to replace *Girls Own* which was to be sold after her arrival but it appears that this may not have happened as planned because there are references to a *Girls Own* operating until *Boys' Own* arrived in 1938.

The Crew of the *Royal Jubilee* possibly taken when she arrived in 1935 or on a subsequent Jubilee day.

(back row left to right)
unknown, Walter Newby.

(front row left to right)
'Tiny' Beesting, J. Newby? Jack Pockley, Bride Pockley, Abe Crawford.

(Bridlington Library)

In May 1936, ten months after *Royal Jubilee* started operating from the harbour, a third new pleasure boat, *New Royal Sovereign,* arrived in Bridlington. Reportedly built in 1929 at Southend-on- Sea it has proved impossible so far to determine by whom though local boat builders Alec Fowler Ltd and John Thorneycroft are possible contenders. *New Royal Sovereign* had plied for hire from Southend until 1936 when she was sold to Albert Butler of Leeds and a consortium of Bridlington fishermen who also owned the *Princess Marina*. The voyage from Southend to Bridlington commenced on Saturday 2nd May 1936 and according to reports at that time she "behaved perfectly and was very steady in the swells", apparently quite good speeds had been achieved despite the fact that the engines, which had just been overhauled, were only run at half speed. A stop was made at Great Yarmouth to refuel and she arrived in Bridlington on Monday 4th May where she was to have a complete renovation carried out in time to operate her first passenger trips from Bridlington during the Whitsuntide holiday.

Described in the local press as "the Queen Mary of the Bridlington pleasure boat fleet" with "a saloon large enough for dancing", the 68grt *New Royal Sovereign* could carry 267 passengers and was fitted with all the latest innovations, such as a wireless, telephone and her own electric light plant. The local press report gave her beam as 20 feet (6m) and her 'length' as 81 feet (24.7m), this 'length' may be incorrect as photographic evidence suggests her overall length was closer to 100 feet (30.5m). At the front of the vessel was a cabin big enough to accommodate the crew of seven, on top of this was an open wheel station bridge, the only protection being a canvas 'dodger' around the bridge front and sides. There was a single funnel aft of the bridge and tall wooden masts towards the bow and stern. Two davit mounted lifeboats were carried aft of the crew cabin on the port and starboard sides and an adequate number of lifejackets were provided for the passengers. She had a flat square stern, twin rudders and was powered by two six-cylinder diesel / oil type engines giving her a maximum speed of ten knots. Below deck she had a large 40 feet

(12.2m) by 20 feet (6.1m) saloon that contained a buffet bar and could be used for dancing or as a café.

New Royal Sovereign in Bridlington Harbour

Following her renovation the *New Royal Sovereign* carried her first Bridlington passengers on Thursday 28th May 1936 when she made a cruise to Flamborough Head and back. Among the passengers were Bridlington Mayor Cllr. A. E. Fligg and his wife. The Mayor took a turn at the wheel on the outward journey under the watchful eye of the Captain, Richard Crawford. Richard had moved over to command the *New Royal Sovereign* and G. Johnson had taken his place as captain of the *Princess Marina*. The crew was reported to be all Bridlington ex-WW1 servicemen. After this inaugural trip *New Royal Sovereign* commenced her pleasure cruises from Bridlington Harbour the most popular being the one shilling (5p) cruises in Bridlington Bay.

This made a total of seven pleasure boats plying for hire at Bridlington in 1936, namely the motor boats *Girls Own*, *Britannia* and *May Morn*, and the pleasure steamers *Yorkshireman*, *Princess Marina*, *Royal Jubilee* and *New Royal Sovereign*. They arrived just in time, for the Whitsuntide holiday in June proved to be the best ever - between Friday and

Tuesday LNER excursion trains carried 33,180 holidaymakers, on Saturday and Sunday 14,000 people passed through Bridlington station, many more arrived in scores of buses and a considerable number arrived by motor car. Fine weather ensured that all the pleasure boats did a roaring trade, Newcomer *New Royal Sovereign* embarked full loads and *Yorkshireman* had queues for its gangway all day.

The next boat to arrive at Bridlington in April 1938 was *Boys' Own* - the second Bridlington pleasure boat to be built by CWG at Beverly.

(Bob Smith)

Boys' Own in Bridlington Harbour in 1938 or 1939

Boys' Own was built in 1938 by CWG of Beverley as yard number 644, official No. 165703, for John, Jim and Walter Newby. She had a gross tonnage of 52 tons and her steel riveted hull was 69 feet (21m) long with a beam of 17 ft (5.2m). Her twin Bergius built Kelvin K4 diesel engines developed 176 horsepower and gave her a speed of 10 knots at 750rpm. The original invoice, dated December 23 1937, gives her cost as £4.650, equal to about £145,000 in today's money. Her hull had a very similar form to that of the *Royal Jubilee*, with a straight stem and cruiser stern and her internal arrangement also followed the same lines as the earlier vessel, with the engine room amidships, a saloon bar forward and a ladies' cabin aft. However, her engine casing was extended upwards to support a flying bridge. Initially the bridge was open, though photographs show that an enclosed wheelhouse was added soon after she entered service. A single ships boat was carried under a pair of davits aft of the bridge on the port side and a canvas awning could be spread to provide covering over the aft passenger area. Plenty of sparred seating was available for her 180 passengers. During Board of Trade trials in the Humber *Boys' Own* was tested three times over a measured mile, twice against the tide and once with it. Her average speed was ten knots. After testing she was approved & registered on the 9th of April 1938 and on her cruises from Bridlington *Boys' Own* was captained by J. R. Newby with W. Newby as engineer.

The penultimate pleasure boat to arrive in Bridlington before the war was named *Miss Mercury*. What she looked like remains something of a mystery as no photographs or postcards have come to light showing her at Bridlington although we have a good description of her from the Bridlington Free Press of Saturday April 9th 1938 which reported her arrival and stated that she was fitted with twin six cylinder Parsons engines each developing 125hp, she had a cruising speed of 16 knots which made her the fastest pleasure boat in Bridlington with the exception of the speedboats. She was 60 feet (18.2m) long with a 14 foot (4.2) beam and a draught of 2 feet 6 inches (0.76m). *Miss Mercury* was licensed to carry 100 passengers, her large saloon, extending from the bridge to the stern, had a telephone connection with the bridge and a radio-gram. It was also reported that *Miss Mercury* was purchased from the Thames Taxi Service by Albert Butler of Leeds and was the third pleasure boat owned by his consortium, they already owned *New Royal Sovereign* and *Princess Marina*, and before her sale she had been used by Miss Jessie Matthews, the famous film star, to travel 30 miles up the Thames every day to the studio where the film 'Sailing Along' was being made. Her journey to Bridlington was far from straightforward. Skippered by Richard Crawford she had left Goole on Sunday April 3rd at 8.30am and arrived off Grimsby at 12.00 noon. A very strong wind was blowing so the skipper decided to go round Spurn Point to see what weather conditions were like in the open sea. They found that a northerly gale was blowing and after sailing three miles past Spurn in a very rough sea they turned around and returned to Grimsby. On Monday the sea conditions were slightly improved and despite heavy seas, *Miss Mercury* made excellent progress, leaving Grimsby at 6.30 in the evening and arriving at Bridlington by 10.00 that night.

On Tuesday April 16th the three Bridlington pleasure boats owned by Albert Butler, *New Royal Sovereign*, *Princess Marina* and *Miss Mercury*, underwent Board of Trade trials in Bridlington Bay. All three boats acted very satisfactorily on their speed trials and manoeuvring tests with *Miss Mercury* showing her superior speed of 16 knots by allowing the other two vessels to get as far as Danes Dyke from the harbour and then starting after them and beating them to Flamborough Head. This was *Miss Mercury's* maiden voyage at Bridlington which was made early in the week to avoid making her maiden trip on a Friday as there is a strong superstition amongst fishermen and boatmen that it is very unlucky to start anything on a Friday.

David Crawford Junior made his first trip as skipper of *Miss Mercury* and the other crew members were well known Bridlington fishermen including Arthur Hutchinson as engineer, Arthur was also the driver of the Tractor used to launch the Bridlington lifeboat. Her first fares were Colonel Kitson, President of the Leeds branch of the British Legion, and Mrs. Kitson.

The final boat to arrive before the start of WW 2 was the *Yorkshire Belle*. *Yorkshire Belle* followed *Boys' Own* on to the stocks in April 1938 at CWG's yard in Beverley as yard number 645, official No. 165707 for R & W Crawford and B & J Pockley of Bridlington and was the third CWG built pleasure boat at Bridlington. *Yorkshire Belle* was 76 feet (23.2m) long with a beam of 17 ft (5.2m) and was powered by the same type of engines as *Boys' Own*, *i.e.* twin Bergius built four cylinder Kelvin K4 diesels developing 176 horsepower which, although she was slightly larger, gave her the same speed of 10 knots. In many respects she was similar to *Royal Jubilee* and *Boys' Own* and like both those vessels, she had a cruiser stern and a similar internal arrangement. The engines and steering were controlled from a flying bridge, which also served as a loading platform for passengers to access the vessel at low tide. In contrast to the earlier vessels, she had streamlined bows with plenty of flare, which gave her a most elegant appearance. Masts were fitted forward and aft and a 12 foot (3.6m) long ships boat was carried on an elevated structure on the port side adjacent to the ladies cabin. The main deck was in Borneo white planking and sparred seating went around most of the deck sides. Three large 'buoyant' seats were carried in centerline positions, two at the bow and one at the stern. Teak skylights on the deck provided natural light to the forward passenger saloon and the aft ladies cabin in the hull, access to these areas being by covered staircases from the main deck. The passenger saloon, finished in mahogany & chromium plate, was just over 20 feet (6.1m) long and ran across the full width of the hull, teak sparred seating covered with leather cushions ran down each side and across one end by the toilet, the forward end of the saloon ended at a mahogany counter from which a bar service was provided. The ladies cabin had wooden bench seats down each side and was just over 9 feet (2.8m) long by 8 feet (2.4m) wide the ends giving access to the staircase and the ladies toilet. Between the passenger saloon and the ladies cabin was the engine room containing two diesel engines and their associated 140 gallon capacity (636.4 litre) fuel tanks.

(Bridlington Library)

The first (1938) *Yorkshire Belle* in Bridlington Harbour

Christened *Yorkshire Belle* by Miss L. Twidle, daughter of the managing director of CWG, on the 7th May 1938, she underwent Board of Trade tests in the Humber and was approved & registered on the 19th of May to carry up to 200 passengers. The journey from

Hull was made with 40 passengers on board and the local newspaper reported that the *Yorkshire Belle,* Bridlington's sixth and latest cruiser, arrived on Thursday, 19th May, 1938. The reporter must have miscounted as in those halcyon pre-war years there could be up to eight pleasure boats operating from Bridlington Harbour at the same time, namely *Yorkshireman, Britannia, May Morn, Princess Marina, New Royal Sovereign, Boys' Own, Miss Mercury* and *Yorkshire Belle.* The *Yorkshire Belle,* with Jack Pockley as the skipper, was to operate from the North Pier, because she was too large to operate from the wooden steps.

The additional pleasure steamers were most welcome for although 1936 had been described as the best ever for visitors to Bridlington, every year afterwards seemed to be better than the previous one, often regardless of the weather. The 1938 arrival of *Yorkshire Belle* and *Boys' Own* allowed two of the existing vessels to be released. The aging *Girls Own* was replaced by *Boys' Own* and *Royal Jubilee* was sold to the St. Mawes Steam Tug and Passenger Co. Ltd in Falmouth Cornwall. Her new owners renamed her *New Roseland* and she was used as the Falmouth to St. Mawes ferry, her subsequent history is detailed in appendix 4. *Royal Jubilee* had only stayed in Bridlington for three years and it is unclear why she left so soon, though it is possible that she was under-powered. Her design speed of 9 knots, as indicated in shipyard records, would have been insufficient to meet the boast quoted in press reports that she would achieve 10-11 knots and keep pace with the *Yorkshireman.* Later vessels of similar size to *Royal Jubilee* would be equipped with more powerful engines that could achieve an extra 1-2 knots. Another factor might have been a bye-law, introduced in March 1938, which could have impeded her operations. Concerned about congestion in the harbour, the authorities ruled that vessels over 70 feet (21.3m) in length should operate from the North Pier, whilst smaller ones should continue to operate from the landing stage at the shoreward end of that pier. Unlike the larger vessels such as *Yorkshireman,* the 74 foot (22.5m) *Royal Jubilee* had no upper deck or flying bridge to receive a gangplank from pier level at low water. In principle, *Royal Jubilee* could have been retrospectively fitted with new engines and an elevated loading platform to overcome these difficulties, but it is possible that the CWG shipyard, which faced a lull in orders in 1938, simply made the consortium a favourable offer to construct new vessels as replacements for the *Royal Jubilee* and the ageing *Girl's Own.*

In July 1938 rumours began to circulate that the owners of the newly arrived *Yorkshire Belle* had applied to transfer her from Bridlington to Scarborough. Apparently they had written to the Harbour Commissioners asking for particulars of running a pleasure boat from Scarborough harbour and had received a reply but did not consider the conditions satisfactory. The Scarborough coble owners had also been perturbed by the rumours and a deputation had visited the Mayor of Scarborough to put before him the Scarborough men's point of view, concern being expressed as to the probable effect on the fishermen's earnings of another pleasure boat with a capacity for 185 passengers plying from Scarborough with two such boats, *Coronia* and *New Royal Lady,* already in operation. The ongoing rumours resulted in Bride H. Pockley, one of the owners of *Yorkshire Belle,* issuing a formal statement to the press that "Yorkshire Belle will not go to Scarborough this year or any other year".

At the end of August, Bridlington Magistrates were occupied for a considerable amount of time with cases involving the pleasure boats *Boys' Own, Princess Marina* and *Miss Mercury* carrying an excess number of passengers, a problem that was to re-occur at various times during the coming years with most of the pleasure boats. Despite the defendants' contending that every precaution was taken and they did not go over their allotted compliment of passengers, fines totalling £60 were imposed. The skippers of *Boys' Own*, (189 passengers – nine too many), *Princess Marina*, (145 passengers – nine too many) and Miss Mercury, (94 passengers – four too many) were fined £15 each. A further summons was brought against the skipper of *Boys' Own for* exceeding the distance limits allowed by his certificate. *Boys' Own* was not allowed to go more than three miles from the shore, and no further north than North Sea Bay (i.e. Thornwick Bay). The senior nautical officer attached to the Hull office was on duty at Bridlington harbour when he saw an advertisement for the *Boys' Own* which stated that the vessel was making a three-hour trip to Bempton, Speeton Cliffs and Filey Bay. A Coastguard officer said the vessel was seen about 3.5 miles (5.6km) north of North Sea Bay. The Bench found the case proved, and a fine of £15 was imposed. The final case that day was against the skipper of the *Yorkshire Belle,* who was summoned for carrying more passengers than his certificate allowed. It was alleged that he landed 195 passengers against the 184 allowed, an excess of 11 passengers. In this case the accurate counting of passengers was complicated by the fact that the *Yorkshire Belle* was anchored outside the harbour owing to the low tide, and that the passengers were disembarked by ferry boats, the passengers being counted by the inspector as they left the ferry boat. It seems that the *Yorkshire Belle* had made six trips that day and on the previous five, passengers had disembarked by the gangplank and when the counts were taken all the numbers were below the certificated number. Given the difficulty in counting passengers leaving several ferry boats at the same time by looking down from the top of the pier and the fact that the two witnesses for the prosecution could not be sure about the actual number of passengers landed, the Bench were of the opinion that there was some doubt in the matter and the case was dismissed.

Occasionally *Yorkshireman* went further afield than her usual trips to Flamborough Head, Bempton Cliffs and Speeton Cliffs and made half day trips to Filey and Hornsea and full day trips to Whitby and Scarborough. One of her day returns to Scarborough was made in early September 1938 with 3½

hours ashore at a cost of 3 shillings and six pence (17.5p) return with first class passengers paying an extra one shilling (5p) for the 'glazed in' boat deck. In autumn when the *Yorkshireman* returned to tug duties on the Humber the glazed screens and the canvas used to cover the rails on the forward and aft boat deck would be removed as would be the canvas awning on the rear deck.

The 1939 season proved as popular has ever despite the gathering war clouds, gas masks and air-raid shelters were in fashion and enrolment of people of both sexes, young and old for National Service had started, compulsory conscription was also introduced for young men between the ages of 18 and 21. *Yorkshire Belle* arrived at Bridlington during the third week in March from Grimsby where she had spent the winter months. She and the other large pleasure boats could not start carrying passengers until the 1st April or the Easter holiday because a little known regulation at that time did not allow them to ply for hire before the 1st April and after the last day in October, but if Easter came before the first of April they could start at Easter. As Easter Sunday in 1939 was the 9th April the pleasure boats could start carrying passengers from the 1st. *Yorkshireman* arrived just before the Easter weekend as usual as did the holiday makers. *Boys' Own* had her first outing of the season on Easter Sunday with a full load of passengers and all the pleasure boats enjoyed a successful Easter as visitors enjoyed what might become their final fling. Whitsuntide in May saw the trend continued with good weather and large crowds. The August Bank Holiday of 1939 saw crowd records broken and the town was crowded with holidaymakers. Thousands came by rail and road, rail traffic was very heavy and there were two mile traffic queues on the roads into Bridlington. East Yorkshire Motor Services reported that their traffic was heavier than last year, all the buses having to be run in duplicate. The sea front presented an animated appearance, and the view was freely expressed that they were the largest crowds ever seen at Bridlington. On Saturday there were 1,500 dancers and 1,076 spectators at the Spa with a further 1,112 present at the Spa Theatre and 470 attending the tea dance. The concerts held in the Spa Royal Hall on Sunday attracted 4,282 and there were 1,928 dancers and 1,170 spectators in the Royal Hall on Monday evening. The Spa Theatre was packed with 1,130 people and a further 850 were at the tea dances. Unprecedented crowds were seen on the Parade and around the harbour, boating maintained its great appeal and proved more popular than ever with the pleasure boats going continually.

Yorkshireman continued with her programmed full day trips to Whitby and Scarborough although by the end of August the threat of war with Germany was greater than ever. Despite all this Council planning continued for the 1940 holiday brochure and efforts were made to continue as normal as far as the resort activities were concerned.

On Friday September 1st Bridlington received over 2,000 evacuee children from Hull on a series of special trains. More trains on Saturday brought a further 2,018 and it was announced that Bridlington would receive a total of 5,000 children plus a further 1,600 to be evacuated throughout the rural district.

The Germans invaded Poland on the 1st September 1939 and at a little after 11.00 am on the 3rd September 1939 the British Prime Minister Neville Chamberlain made the following broadcast:

> *"I am speaking to you from the Cabinet Room at 10 Downing Street.*
>
> *This morning the British Ambassador in Berlin handed the German Government a final note stating that, unless we hear from them by 11 o'clock that they were prepared at once to withdraw their troops from Poland, a state of war would exist between us. I have to tell you now that no such undertaking has been received, and that consequently this country is at war with Germany".*

7
The War Years

The loss of the New Royal Sovereign and Yorkshire Belle

With the exception of *Yorkshireman* all pleasure boat activity ceased at noon on the 3rd September 1939 when war was declared. It had little immediate impact because the season was over and *Yorkshireman* had returned to Hull by the 9th September anyway, where she was requisitioned for war duties by the Ministry of Shipping on 6th October 1939. *New Royal Sovereign* had also been requisitioned in September by the Royal Navy. On the 2nd October the town council officially cancelled the forthcoming 1939 Sea Angling Festival and began to refuse license applications and renewals for speedboats. As the country entered the so called 'phoney war' period the Ministry of Labour set up a Committee to advise on how to ensure that industrial workers on war-time production could take a holiday. The Committee advocated spreading the holiday period from May to October and appealed to local authorities, employers and trade unions to arrange meetings to discuss local arrangements which included advice to holidaymakers to bring their ration books with them. *Boys' Own* was requisition by the Royal Navy on the 16th November 1939 and on the 23rd November *Yorkshire Belle* was also requisitioned by the Royal Navy, both vessels being used for harbour duties as boom defence vessels and mine patrol duties. The war at sea however was not 'phoney' and one of the first casualties to be brought into Bridlington Harbour was the 1914 built Grimsby trawler *Erillus*, registered GY234 for the Consolidated Steam Fishing & Ice Co. she survived the war and was not scrapped until 1955, in January 1940 the Newbigin Steam Shipping Companies 1910 built steamer SS *Gripfast* attempted to enter Bridlington Harbour after being damaged by bombs and machine gun fire when 10 miles off Flamborough Head, the attempt failed and she ran aground on the South Sands near the pier. She was re-floated and re-entered service but was bombed and sunk in 1942.

On the 6th March 1940 the fishing boats Guiding Light and Albatross were attacked off Bridlington by three German aircraft, later that month petrol rationing was in operation, but despite this the Bridlington Fishermen and Boatmen Society had applied for and obtained enough petrol to cover the Easter holiday period. Throughout the Easter weekend thousands flocked to Bridlington, large crowds assembled on the sea front and there was an almost constant stream of pedestrians walking along the cliff tops to Sewerby although evenings were spent on indoor entertainment as 'strolling' proved difficult in the blackout. Motor traffic was very heavy considering the petrol rationing and the increased numbers of cyclist was very apparent. As usual the pier and harbour proved an extremely popular haunt for the holiday-makers and there was a good deal of pleasure boating although it has proved impossible to determine which pleasure boats were operating but it was probably only *Girls Own, May Morn, Britannia* and *Princess Marina* because *Yorkshireman, Boys' Own, New Royal Sovereign* and *Yorkshire Belle* had all been requisitioned for war duties.

Any thoughts that the successful Easter augured well for the future were soon shattered when at the end of March 1940 the Town Council was informed by the Flag Officer Humber that an order banning the sailing of pleasure boats from Bridlington Bay would shortly be introduced, and it was likely that it would be extended to cover the whole of the East Coast. This 'anticipated' order caused great consternation to the boatmen and much confusion to the authorities as to whether an order was in force or not and by April 6th the Mayor of Bridlington stated that the council were not entitled to act on anticipation or supposition and on the advice of the towns legal advisor nothing would be done until an order was received from an appropriate authority. This was only a brief respite however and by the 8th April the appropriate orders had been received and the council confirmed "that all existing licences issued by the council in respect of pleasure boats and vessels be revoked forthwith". For the pleasure boat operators' things could only get worse, by May 17th the 1940 Whitsuntide holiday had been cancelled and the whole concept of holidays by the sea had to be rethought and was replaced by 'Holidays at Home'. By the end of the month navigation orders were in force which severely restricted the movement of all vessels and by the end of June Defence Regulations were in force which among other things fixed 10.00pm as the hour of closing of all places of entertainment. By this time the effects of the banning of pleasure boat activity was largely academic as there were no holidaymakers and a shortage of men to crew any boat because the younger Bridlington fishermen and boatmen were being called up for service in the Royal Navy or joining the Merchant Navy. Any boatmen who were in the RNR and RNVR were being drafted into the Royal Navy and the Naval Patrol Service was being formed with an age limit of 55 and this creamed off more fisherman and boatmen to minesweepers and patrol vessels.

As the war situation deteriorated and the BEF retreated to Dunkirk, operation Dynamo, the evacuation of the army from Dunkirk, was initiated during late May 1940 with thousands of different types of vessels, including pleasure boats, congregating in various harbours, including Bridlington, to go to Dunkirk if needed.

At Bridlington the boatmen gathered on the Fish Dock and Walter Newby found that he was issued with the same type of rifle that he had used in WW1, eager to prove his prowess he took aim at the 'fish' weather vane on the North pier and put a bullet through its tail – the bullet hole can still be seen today.

(Arthur Newby)

Arthur and Neil Newby with the weather vane
'ventilated' by their father Walter

The boats gathered at Bridlington were not called upon for the Dunkirk evacuation and none of them are officially recorded as participating. Two pleasure boats with local connections did go to Dunkirk and could be the basis of the rumours that Bridlington pleasure boats took part, the boats that went to Dunkirk were *Brit* (often confused with *Britannia*) as HMS *Watchful* and *Oulton Belle* (confused with *Yorkshire Belle*). *Oulton Belle* eventually became the *Regal Lady* at Scarborough and to add to the name confusion a previous *Brit* had become the Princess Marina at Bridlington – the pleasure boat names *Brit*, *Britannia* and *Belle* often became mixed up in people's recollections.

In August Bridlington was declared a 'Defence Area', the beach was mined, the seafront cordoned off with barbed wire, road blocks placed at strategic positions, a curfew imposed and access to the harbour severely restricted. By now the Skipsea bombing and gunnery range had closed and the RAF marine craft boats in Bridlington harbour were on continual standby for Air-Sea Rescue (ASR) duties. Plans were being formulated to mine the piers, install flame throwers and sink a block ship across the harbour entrance. The military authorities took over complete technical control of the harbour and the plans were put into effect. The mining of the seaward end of the North Pier was thought unnecessary and was replaced by digging a cavity at the shore end near the steps where a hole was dug below the level of the sea bed and a tunnel extended for 20 yards (18.3m), filled with high explosive and fused to be detonated from a shop near Crane Wharf. The South Pier was mined in a similar manner and detonated from the RAF watch tower on the fish quay. Four flamethrowers were worked from a shelter on Crane Wharf which was made into a fuel store and engine house with two pumping engines. Two flame thrower nozzles were installed on the North Pier, one of which could be directed outside the harbour entrance, the third nozzle was on the wooden jetty of Crane Wharf camouflaged as an upturned boat and the fourth nozzle was by the Harbour Masters House disguised as a water butt. An old barge was moored near the seaward end of the South Pier ready to be towed across the harbour entrance and sunk as a block ship should the need arise.

The North Sea now became a very dangerous place with mines being laid by enemy submarines and aircraft at every opportunity. In naval matters Bridlington came under the Humber sub-command of Nore Command and to tackle the menace of the mines, naval mine clearance teams were established at Bridlington, Mablethorpe, Brightlingsea and Chatham with the Bridlington based naval team tackling many mines along the nearby coast. The east coast began to suffer from numerous air raids and in August the Oberon Café and adjoining baths on the harbourside were destroyed by bombs. Later that month at 0250 hours on Friday, 23rd August 1940, a lone Ju88 of KG30 made a low level attack on Bridlington Harbour dropping four high explosive bombs. The first bomb struck the 68grt *New Royal Sovereign* and blew her to pieces, luckily no crew were on board. Parts of her engines were found on the south beach along with lamp standards from the south pier. The second bomb dropped on the jetty, failed to explode and ricocheted through the bottom of the coble *Blue Jacket*. The third bomb wrecked Foley's Cafe in Prince Street next to the harbour and damaged Woolworths next door. The fourth bomb demolished the Cock & Lion public house in Prince Street. The following morning on Germany's propaganda radio, Lord Haw-Haw announced the destruction of the Royal Navy battleship *HMS Royal Sovereign* following a raid on Bridlington by Luftwaffe bombers. *New Royal Sovereign* appears to have been the only former pleasure boat remaining at Bridlington by August 1940 the others being either laid up or requisitioned. *Girls Own, May Morn* and *Miss Mercury* seem to have disappeared, whether sold or broken up is not recorded and their wartime activities are unknown. *Britannia* and *Princess Marina* 'went away' during the war, to where and for what purpose has not been recorded. There are unconfirmed reports that *Princess Marina* was fitted with a deck gun and operated on the Thames. *Yorkshireman* was at Grimsby for use on towage and rescue services and *Royal Jubilee*, now *New Roseland* was being used as a barrage balloon vessel in the Bristol Channel. *Boys' Own* was fitted with a six pounder gun on the forecastle and anti-aircraft guns on the Bridge. *Boys' Own* probably operated initially on the River Humber but at some time the Navy sold or transferred her to the Royal Army Service Corps (R.A.S.C.) and she is believed to have operated on the Tees and Tyne as well. *Yorkshire Belle* was probably armed in a similar fashion to *Boys' Own* and operated out of Grimsby or Hull.

Early in 1940 The Bridlington branch of the British legion adopted the newly built Bangor Class Minesweeper *HMS Bridlington* (J65) a ship that was to have a close relationship with the town for many years.

With the increased enemy activity the authorities decided that evacuating children to Bridlington was not such a good, or safe, idea after all, and the evacuees were rapidly returned home or dispersed to adjoining rural areas.

On the 20th March 1941 the 25 ton Grimsby registered GY161 wooden fishing vessel *Joan Margaret* was being used by the Merchant Navy as a civil defence boat No T124 for spotting mines in the Humber Estuary. At that time the Admiralty considered that a wooden hulled boat would be safe - they presumed wrongly and at 8 pm the *Joan Margaret* hit a mine near the Cleeness Light Float, and blew up. Of the six man crew from Filey, four were killed instantly, one died later from his injuries and one survived because he had gone topside for a smoke and was blown clear. One of the boats that rushed to help was the former Bridlington Pleasure boat *Yorkshire Belle* with three more Filey men on board. Three weeks later on 11th April 1941 the 56grt *Yorkshire Belle* sank with all hands after an underwater explosion (believed to be caused by a magnetic mine) 3½ cables (640m) from Haile Sand Fort in the river Humber.

In May the Yorkshire Yacht Building and Engineering Company leased land on Langdales Wharf to build boats for the war effort. Activity at the harbour mainly involved RN vessels, RAF marine craft and fishing boats that were tightly controlled in where and when they could fish though June brought some relaxation in the regulations affecting inshore fishing.

Towards the end of 1941 Bridlington and district held a Warship Week with the aim of 'buying' HMS *Bridlington*. The scheme worked by people 'lending' money to the government to buy weapons to win the war. The initial target was £133,000 and at the end of Warship Week the figure invested was £293,762 - more than twice the original target, or enough to buy *H.M.S. Bridlington* and one of her sister ships. £48,060 of the money invested was contributed by the 20 villages around Bridlington and included £1,000 from the Bridlington Rural District Council on behalf of the

WARSHIP WEEK, November 29th to December 6th

HELP TO BUY

H.M.S. "BRIDLINGTON"

LEND TO DEFEND. The Government asks you to LEND your money, upon which you will be paid interest, for weapons to win the war.

Bridlington is set to raise £136,000. the full cost of H.M.S. "Bridlington." We must not fail. Let us show by how much we can surpass this figure. Remember, this is an APPEAL. It might have been a DEMAND— "GIVE TO LIVE."

Take your savings to any Bank, the Post Office, or one of the Selling Centres.

THIS SPACE IS GIVEN BY:

R. Allen & Co. Ltd.	F. E. Gray & Co. Ltd.	Quarton's
W. Foster Brigham	Holtby, White & Co. Ltd.	Regal Cinema
Carlton's Ltd.	Lounge Cinema	P. H. Smallwood
H. Davis & Co. Ltd.	Wm. Neal & Son Ltd.	Winter Gardens

rural parishes. Nearly nine months later in September 1942 permanent mementoes were exchanged between Bridlington Borough and Rural District and *H.M.S. Bridlington* at a gathering in the reception room of the Town Hall. A plaque bearing the coat of arms of Bridlington was presented by the Mayor (Alderman T. D. Fenby) on behalf of the town and rural district to Lieutenant P. J. Bayne R.N. who represented the Lieutenant Commanding, officers and ships company of *H.M.S, Bridlington*. In return, Lieutenant Bayne presented mounted replicas of the ship's badge to the Mayor and to Councillor D. R. Jackson, the Chairman of the Rural District Council.

Wartime security, restrictions, rationing and uncertainty continued through the following years and it was not until December 1944 when the Home Guard were stood down that people felt that the worse was over. A sign of a return to normality came in February 1945 with the announcement that pleasure boating was now permissible in Bridlington Bay, after being prohibited since the outbreak of war. This followed a notification from R.N. Naval Base Headquarters "that there are now no objections by the naval or military authorities to pleasure boats plying for hire within the limits of the Bay" however the notification stated that boats may be used only during daylight hours and passengers may be embarked and disembarked only within the harbour. This last condition rendered the permitted pleasure boating academic since the harbour was in no fit state to accept passengers as it was still 'mined' and in need of extensive repairs which the Piers and Harbour Commissioners could not afford - and if they could there was nobody to do it! Later in the month the restriction on pleasure sailing at Scarborough, Filey, Bridlington and Whitby was removed but with the same conditions regarding the hours of daylight and embarking and disembarking from harbours.

Suddenly the war in Europe was over and on VE day, 8th May 1945, flags and bunting were displayed in every street, business premises and the Town Hall. Bridlington's Victory parade took place a week later and the last POW's returned home in June. Work on returning the harbour to its peace time duties was still held up as the claim against the Military and Admiralty for the cost of deferred maintenance work and the removal of defensive structures was still being pursued. The North Pier remained closed to the public although the barbed wire had been removed from the steps and approaches. The South pier and fish quay had been opened and was becoming busier with more boats coming in. Several applications for speedboat licenses had been made but the Bridlington Piers and Harbour Commissioners considered them a danger to small craft and other users of the harbour and decided that no speedboats would be allowed to ply from the harbour or any place over which the Commissioners had jurisdiction.

The Yorkshire Yacht Building and Engineering Company on Langdales Wharf announced that it had built 112 vessels, many of them being Motor Fishing Vessels (MFV's) and installed 131 engines. It was also disclosed that vessels from the Bridlington based marine craft unit, operating in the ASR role, had saved over thirty lives during the war. Unfortunately there is very little known about the activities of the Bridlington pleasure boats that were moved away or requisitioned and of the ten pleasure boats that operated in Bridlington in 1938, two boats, *New Royal Sovereign* and *Yorkshire Belle* had been sunk, three boats, *Girls Own*, *May Morn* and *Miss Mercury* did not return to operating at Bridlington. *Yorkshireman* was still operating as a tug on the Humber and *Royal Jubilee*, as *New Roseland*, had returned to service as the Falmouth to St. Mawes ferry. Only three pleasure boats, namely *Britannia*, *Princess Marina*, and *Boys' Own* returned to Bridlington and were available for pleasure trips when these started up again in 1946.

THE SCREW DRIVEN PLEASURE BOATS

The location of the pleasure boats during the war are summarized in the following table

Vessel Name	1939 -1945
Girls Own	Location unknown - did not return to Bridlington after the war.
Britannia	Went away – activities unknown
May Morn	Location unknown - did not return to Bridlington after the war.
Yorkshireman	Requisitioned for war service at Hull and sent to Grimsby for use on towage and rescue services
Princess Marina	Went away – activities unknown
Royal Jubilee	Requisitioned for war service as *New Roseland* at Falmouth and used as a barrage balloon vessel in the Bristol Channel
New Royal Sovereign	Requisitioned for war service and sunk in Bridlington Harbour in 1940
Miss Mercury	Location unknown - did not return to Bridlington after the war.
Boys' Own	Requisitioned for war service as a boom defence vessel. Later with the R.A.S.C. on the river Tees, Tyne and Humber
Yorkshire Belle	Requisitioned for war service for patrol duties and as a boom defence vessel. sunk in the River Humber in 1941

ROLL OF HONOUR
FOR THE CREW OF THE *"YORKSHIRE BELLE"*
LOST ON THE 11th APRIL 1941

ERNEST WALTER JOHNSON

Petty Officer, R/JX 224902, H.M.S. Yorkshire Belle Royal Navy. 11 April 1941. Age 30. Son of Walter and Maud Johnson of Hull; husband of Beatrice Annie Johnson of Hull.

WILLIAM HERBERT HARRISON

Stoker 1st Class, R/KX 112255, H.M.S. Yorkshire Belle, Royal Navy. 11 April 1941. Age 21.

ROBERT McILVAR

Rigger, D/J 81281, H.M. Yacht Yorkshire Belle, Royal Navy. 11 April 1941. Age 40. Son of George and Susan Caldwell Mcllvar; husband of Martha Mcllvar, of Renfrew.

WILLIAM HENRY BENNETT

Rigger's Mate, , R/JX 192712, H.M. Yacht Yorkshire Belle, Royal Navy. 11 April 1941. Age 22. Son of William and Mary Bennett, of Rosyth, Fife.

DANIEL GIBSON

Rigger's Mate, R/JX 180005, H.M. Boom Defence Vessel Yorkshire Belle, Royal Navy. 11 April 1941. Age 32. Son of Mr. and Mrs. Michael Gibson; husband of Catherine Gibson, of Glasgow

JAMES STEPHEN RICHARD FAGG

Cook (S), C/MX 65006, H.M.S. Yorkshire Belle, Royal Navy. 11 April 1941. Age 23. Son of James and Suzan Fagg; husband of Ena Ethel Fagg, of London

GEORGE WORTHINGTON BUTTRISS

Able Seaman, R/JX 180734, H.M.S. Yorkshire Belle, Royal Navy. 11 April 1941. Age 26. Son of George Henry and Alice Mary Buttriss, of Jarrow-on-Tyne, Co. Durham.

ALBERT THOMPSON

Able Seaman, C/JX 222063, H.M. Yacht Yorkshire Belle, Royal Navy. 11 April 1941. Age 24. Son of Herbert and Alice Thompson; husband of Edna Thompson, of Hull, Yorkshire.

8
Post War Recovery

Boys Own and *Yorkshireman* are joined by *Titlark, Bridlington Queen, Thornwick* and a new *Yorkshire Belle*

After the war things were slow to recover, by Easter (April 21st) 1946 the harbour defenses at Bridlington had not been cleared, however just over one month later on May 25th the military authorities had given the Harbour Commissioners a clearance certificate showing both piers were now free from explosives and could be re-opened to the public. The only pleasure boats known to have been at Bridlington in 1946 were *Britannia, Princess Marina, Boys' Own* and a new boat *Titlark,* there is no evidence that *May Morn* and *Miss Mercury* returned to Bridlington though their whereabouts or fate is unknown.

(Authors collection)

Bridlington Harbour 1946
(left to right) *Britannia, Titlark, Princess Marina* and *Boys' Own*

With rationing still in operation and fuel restricted it was August Bank holiday before the holiday visitors arrived in appreciable numbers, 12,000 arriving on Saturday alone, 26 special excursion trains were run, bringing holidaymakers from Leeds, Sheffield, Bradford, Manchester, Liverpool and Leicester, between 800 and 900 emergency ration cards were issued by the Food Office for visitors stopping in Bridlington.. Pleasure boating was much in evidence and some pleasure boat owners let the holiday crowds' enthusiasm for pleasure trips overrule their licensed numbers and the owners of the cobles *Primrose, Francis* and the pleasure boat *Britannia* were later fined for having too many people on their boats.

On its de-commissioning in February 1946, *Boys' Own* was offered back to its original owners, the Newby brothers. Only John was interested, so the boat was sold back to John Newby and three additional shareholders, Fred Milner, David 'Boyzie' Crawford and Bobby Fisher. The boat was sailed back to Bridlington from Greenock, Scotland, by Fred Milner and 'Boyzie' Crawford. On the 7th March she was returned to CWG for conversion back to a pleasure steamer. The concrete at the forecastle was removed (this had been the support for the gun). The cast iron ingots (used as ballast for the Anti-aircraft guns and to restore the trim) were removed from the stern bilges. All life-raft seating and side seating had to be replaced, stern awnings refitted and a new bar and tables fitted into the forward saloon. Engines had to be stripped and checked before she was ready for public service. A small plaque was originally fitted under the bridge, supplied by the Ministry of Defence, confirming that the Boys Own had shot down an enemy aircraft, the whereabouts of this plaque is not known. The conversion work was completed by the 15th April and she returned to Bridlington, with a slightly reduced capacity for up to 155 passengers, in time to make pleasure trips during the August Bank holiday.

The newcomer *Titlark* had a rather convoluted history - "Bridlington Welcomes Boat Which Scarborough and Filey Spurned" was the headline in the Bridlington Free Press of Saturday August 10th 1946 when it reported the arrival of the *Titlark 1* in the harbour. *Titlark 1* and her sister *Titlark 2* were built by the Skylark Shipyard of Jake Bolson and Son of Bournemouth in 1936 and 1937 respectively and operated by them for cruises from Bournemouth. They were 70ft (21.35m) long and fitted with Parson's petrol/paraffin engines driving twin screws. They could carry 150 passengers, saloons, bar/buffet and toilets were installed and radio was also fitted. After war service, *Titlark 1* was sold to Holiday Camp Cruises Ltd., a subsidiary of Butlins, who held a two thirds controlling interest, the other one-third share was held by Bernard Foote the skipper of the boat. Her presence in Bridlington was the result of a rather convoluted story involving Filey, Scarborough and Butlins. It had initially been intended to operate *Titlark 1* from Filey, but subtle pressure was applied by the local mariners against the *Titlark* as the approaches most suitable to the boat for going inshore were also those most favored for crab fishing. Fleets of crab pots would have been an obstacle to operations with the possibilities of fouling arid compensation to fishermen. The Board of Trade authorities at Hull agreed and would not grant a licence on account of inadequate berthing and landing facilities at Filey. They did however grant a licence to operate from Scarborough and *Titlark 1* moved there but the motor boat owners at Scarborough staged a strike in protest at *Titlark 1* being granted a licence to ply for hire at Scarborough, they resumed normal duties next day but a petition signed by nearly 50 boatmen was presented to the Harbour Commissioners Committee and a similar one went to the Mayor for submission to the Watch Committee. Although *Titlark 1* possessed a Board of Trade licence it was the Harbour Commissioners who were responsible for berthing and landing facilities and they took legal advice on their responsibilities. Events were moving very quickly and a week after the outbreak of opposition at Scarborough *Titlark 1* was offered for sale by the directors of Holiday Camp Cruises Ltd., Bernard Foote the skipper of the boat indicated his willingness to operate the *Titlark 1* if any purchasers came forward and appropriate facilities made available. *Titlark 1* was then sold to a number of Scarborough individuals and she quickly left the scene of controversy and sailed to Bridlington. At Bridlington she was skippered by James Newby, one of Bridlington's best known boatmen, who 'intimated' that the *Titlark 1* was still owned by Scarborough people, but was being sailed by Bridlington men on a share basis. The share system was itself rather complicated and came about because the owners and men of seven Bridlington motor cobles felt that they could not compete with the larger boats and decided to take an interest in *Titlark 1*. James Newby was the skipper and three other men from the cobles formed the crew, the 'owners' took a share of the profits and the remainder was pooled along with the takings from the seven cobles and there was a share-out among the Bridlington men concerned. John Moorhouse of Bridlington went on a *Titlark* cruise and remembers that the only protection around her low stern was a sort of net fence and that a pair of aspidistra like plants stood in pots on either side of the entrance to the saloon. At the end of the 1946 summer season *Titlark 1* departed Bridlington and did not return, her subsequent history is detailed in appendix 4.

Yorkshireman had returned to Hull when the war ended and was used for general towing duties. The large amount of post war towing work available meant that *Yorkshireman* did not return to Bridlington until 31st May 1947 and began pleasure trips the next day, Whitsunday. However not everyone was pleased by her return and on the 10th May, before her arrival, the local press reported a protest by the Bridlington Fishermen's and Boatmen's Society that whilst coal rationing was still in force and their coal supply was restricted, *Yorkshireman* had coal for pleasure cruises despite the fact that there were plenty of local motor boats that could carry passengers with more due to arrive later in the year. Despite all this *Yorkshireman* quickly proved to be as popular as ever and settled into her pre-war itinerary of running pleasure trips throughout the summer months and towing on the Humber in winter.

In 1947 *Boys' Own* was advertised as cruising daily at 10.15am, 2.15pm and 6.15 pm to Flamborough Head, Silex and Thornwick Bays and Flamborough

Your Favourite — The

BOYS' OWN

Cruises Daily at 10-15 a.m., 2-15 p.m. and 6-15 p.m. for Flamborough Head, Silex and Thornwick Bays, Lighthouse and Caves.

Fully Licensed Bar.   Ladies' Saloon.
Sheltered accommodation for all passengers.
Skipper **David Crawford**, a member of Bridlington Lifeboat crew

Lighthouse and Caves. Facilities on offer included a fully licensed bar, ladies saloon and 'sheltered accommodation for all passengers'. Her skipper David Crawford was a member of the Bridlington lifeboat crew, as was Frank Johnson who ran the *Princess Marina* which offered similar times, destinations and facilities.

By 1947 *Britannia* was licensed for 100 passengers and her net registered tonnage was recorded as 10 tons. She seems to have changed ownership at some time, either pre or post WW2? and in 1947 was reported as owned by Robert Ingram of Sheffield.

Ownership of the large pleasure boats represented a considerable financial outlay that was generally beyond the resources of a single individual. One solution was to form consortiums involving local people interested in investing in the pleasure boat trade. Consortiums spread the cost of buying, operating and maintaining the boats and provided a source of manpower with a wide knowledge of seamanship, the local area and its weather. Although a consortium 'owned' a vessel, very often it was only a single name that appeared on the build, or purchase order, and on the licence. The owner could also be the skipper, or the skipper and the crew could be consortium members or independently hired. Some consortium members could be 'sleeping' partners or actively involved in running the boat.

Consortium members could 'sell' their interests to other individuals or the consortium could be expanded or reduced in numbers. With all these possible permutations it is impossible to state with any certainty that the named 'owner(s)' of the large pleasure boats were the only owners or were acting for a consortium.

Two new pleasure boats arrived early in 1947, *Bridlington Queen* from Moseley, Surry and a new *Yorkshire Belle* from CWG at Beverley.

Bridlington Queen had been laid down towards the end of the war as a standard Admiralty hull designed Motor Fishing Vessel (MFV). After the war the uncompleted MFV became surplus to requirements and was adapted by Watercraft Ltd., East Molesey, near Hampton Court on the river Thames as a shallow draft pleasure boat for Robert Ingram who also owned *Britannia*.

She was launched on Thursday 22 May 1947, co-incidentally the day before the launch of the new *Yorkshire Belle* at Beverly, and had started cruising from Bridlington by August that year

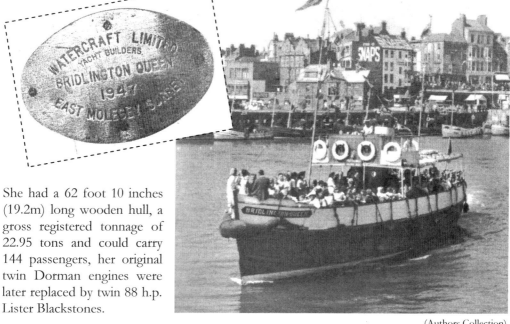

She had a 62 foot 10 inches (19.2m) long wooden hull, a gross registered tonnage of 22.95 tons and could carry 144 passengers, her original twin Dorman engines were later replaced by twin 88 h.p. Lister Blackstones.

(Authors Collection)

Bridlington Queen in her 'open bridge' configuration

In her original configuration *Bridlington Queen* had a dark natural wood finish with white top and an open bridge, similar to the original layout of the *Boys' Own* and the 1938 *Yorkshire Belle*, Her skipper at Bridlington was the well known boatman and lifeboat man Walter Newby. Soon after her arrival two alterations were made - a barge-style wheelhouse with distinctive backwards-sloping windows replaced the open bridge and a wooden rubbing strip was added to her hull to prevent chafing by other vessels moored alongside her, usually *Boys' Own*. In the 1950's.her original dark natural wood finish was changed to an all white painted scheme

The other new arrival, *Yorkshire Belle,* was built by CWG of Beverley as yard number 793, official No. 181302, for Bride Hall Pockley. She was launched on Wednesday 22nd May 1947 and registered on Thursday 30th May. With a registered length of 80 feet (24.4m) and a beam of 19 feet (5.8m), she was slightly longer and broader than the first *Yorkshire Belle*. The twin Crossley 8WM6 diesel engines, each developing 120 bhp, were controlled from a covered wheelhouse, the top of which (The Upper Bridge) served as a loading platform for passengers to access the vessel from the pier. The engine exhaust was piped aft and exited near the stern just above the waterline, the funnel was a dummy. Two tall masts were fitted and amidships her hull sides were carried upwards to the level of the wheelhouse deck. She had an elegant streamlined flared bow and a top speed of 10.3 knots. Like her predecessor she carried a 12 foot (3.6m) long ships boat on the port side, sparred seating around the deck sides and three 'buoyant' seats in centerline positions. Deck skylights provided natural light to the passenger saloon and the ladies cabin below. The passenger saloon was just over 20 feet (6.1m) long and sparred seating with leather cushions ran around three sides, the forward end of the saloon ended at an elegant curved bar counter that could be closed off by a roller shutter.

(Authors Collection)

The 1947 built *Yorkshire Belle* in Bridlington Bay in the early 1950's

The ladies cabin was 12 feet (3.6m) long with sparred seating and leather cushions around the sides. The passenger saloon and the ladies cabin both had toilets fitted. The engine room, containing two diesel engines and two 140 gallon capacity (636.4 litres) diesel oil tanks, was located in the 13 x 18 foot (4 x 5.5 m) area between the passenger saloon and the ladies cabin. Weather protection for passengers on the aft deck was provided by a canvas awning spread over steel framework carried aft from the funnel to the stern. Following her registration, *Yorkshire Belle* arrived at Bridlington on the weekend of the 31st May / 1st June 1947 and quickly proved a winner. Licensed to carry 207 passengers she was very popular and everyone wanted to go on the 'new' boat. The adverts for the new *Yorkshire Belle* came out early with the similar times, destinations and facilities as *Boys' Own* and *Princess Marina,* but also claiming the title of 'Bridlington's Newest, Fastest Pleasure Cruiser'. Some obviously went to print before she arrived as they depict the 1938 built *Yorkshire Belle* that was lost in the war.

In August 1947 the boating inspectors claimed that the Master had allowed on board 353 passengers, and the case came to court later in October when a summons was brought against Bride Hall Pockley, that on 14 August being the master of the *Yorkshire Belle* he received on board more passengers than was laid down by the steamer's certificate. The boating inspector employed by the Bridlington Corporation claimed that on 14 August he counted the passengers by means of an automatic counter as they disembarked and found the number of people to be 353. When Mr. Pockley junior came ashore he mentioned it to him but did not speak to the defendant Bride Hall Pockley. During the evidence it was revealed that the passengers disembarked from two gangways four yards (3.6m) apart and it was suggested that the inspector had made a bad error in counting passenger discharging from two gangways. The defending solicitor also said the case must fail because no evidence had been given that Bride Pockley was the master of the vessel (although he was one of the owners). In fact his son John Cross Pockley was the master on that day. The case was dismissed.

Yorkshireman was used as a grandstand at the Harbour Water Sports in August 1947, being moored between the jetty and the pier, with the other five large pleasure boats, *Britannia, Boys' Own, Princess Marina, Bridlington Queen* and *Yorkshire Belle* located around the sports area. *Yorkshireman* took passengers on board at 2/6p (about £3 today) a seat to watch the events, one of which was a demonstration of how frogmen operated during the war by Peter Williams from Butlins Ltd, using the *Yorkshireman* as his 'target'. August 1947 seems to have also been a busy time for *Boys' Own,* the collier *Sherwood* collided with the cargo ship *Kindat* off Flamborough Head and the skipper of *Boys' Own* Richard Crawford went out to help, two crewmen from *Boys' Own,* A Purvis and W Newby, were put aboard and assisted in bringing her safely into harbour, the *Kindat* was relatively undamaged and continued to her destination.

The Whitsuntide holiday in May 1948 had ideal weather and although petrol was still rationed and 'pleasure motoring' banned, the crowds came to Bridlington with over 80 motor coaches being counted on the Whit Saturday in Hilderthorpe car park by the railway station. Many of the holiday makers were day trippers, a relatively new phenomenon that would become increasingly popular in the future.

The last new pleasure boat to arrive in Bridlington was the *Thornwick* in 1948. *Thornwick* was of steel construction and built at the shipbuilding yard of D. E. Scarr Ltd. in Howdendyke for Col. Albert Butler of Scholes Village near Leeds. The launching ceremony in December 1947 was performed by Mrs. Butler the wife of the owner.

When she arrived at Bridlington *Thornwick* was, with the exception of Yorkshireman, the largest pleasure craft operating from the harbour. She had a gross registered tonnage of 126 tons, was 100 feet (30.7m) long, had a beam of 21 feet (6.4m) and a top speed of 11 knots. She could carry 337 passengers and safety equipment included lifejackets for every passenger, buoyant seats / rafts and a 24 passenger life boat carried on the port side. The ship's twin Gardner 8L43 engines, each of which developed 150 hp. at 900 revolutions, were controlled from an open bridge and had a story all their own. Although Albert Butler was given a permit to have the *Thornwick* built there was no permit available for engines, so he bought Harbour Defence Motor Launch (HDML) Launch 1305 which was then 'lying in

Valetta Harbour' (Malta). He set sail for England with a crew of five and home waters were reached after many adventures including a sudden storm in the Bay of Biscay that almost ended the voyage. The engines were overhauled by the makers and installed in the *Thornwick* together with the Gardner IL2 engine for emergency lighting and water. Flat out the engines consumed 7 gallons of fuel an hour. By a strange coincidence HDML Launch 1305 survived the loss of her engines, was restored and re-engined with 225hp gray marine engines (Detroit Diesels).

Thornwick arrived at Bridlington on Saturday June 26 1948 to begin her pleasure boat activities and was granted plying rights between Hull and Whitby. She originally had a black hull, copying the colour schemes of the *Yorkshireman* and the great ocean liners. This soon gave way to a white colour scheme which she then retained throughout her career at Bridlington. Facilities onboard included a main saloon, a tea saloon and a ladies' cabin, her hull had five watertight bulkheads and she could be easily recognised by her two decks and distinctive twin funnels.

(Bridlington Library)

Thornwick in her initial black hull colour scheme

She usually carried a crew of seven and over the years her crew included many well known mariners including the mate Frank Johnson who was also bowman of the Bridlington Lifeboat in 1948. Some of her skippers included George Colebridge, a retired sea captain from Hull, Ken Lester, Gordon Fox and G Johnson, former skipper of the *Princess Marina*. *Thornwick* was a replacement for the sunken *New Royal Sovereign* and the existing *Princess Marina* and around the time of her arrival at Bridlington in June 1948, *Princess Marina* was sold to Sea Cruises (Whitby) Ltd and sailed from Whitby. Whether *Princess Marina* departed

Bridlington before or after the arrival of Thornwick is unclear and the subsequent history of *Princess Marina* is detailed in appendix 4. *Thornwick* commenced running a programme of excursion trips to Scarborough and Whitby with shorter trips to Flamborough Head, Speeton and Filey Bay. The Scarborough and Whitby destinations included time ashore and a licensed bar and a snack bar were available on all cruises. There was plenty of covered accommodation and passengers could use the radio telephone if needed.

The popular BBC radio programme 'Beside the Seaside' was broadcast from Bridlington in July 1948 and among those interviewed was Richard Crawford the skipper of the *Boys' Own* pleasure boat.

By 1949 wartime restrictions were being relaxed and with the Easter holiday being three weeks later and good weather over the weekend the visitors came to Bridlington in large numbers. The pleasure boats were extremely popular with all of them going out 'well laden'. An added attraction in the bay was the town's namesake ship, His Majesty's Air Force Vessel (HMAFV) *Bridlington*, formerly the minesweeper HMS *Bridlington* which was adopted by Bridlington and District during WW2. The harbour was now a very busy place, particularly around the landing stage known as the 'broad steps' which was used for loading and unloading from rowing boats, pleasure cobles, speedboats and ferry boats. With six pleasure boats, *Britannia, Boys' Own, Bridlington Queen, Yorkshire Belle, Thornwick* and the ever popular pleasure tug *Yorkshireman*, all operating from the harbour space was at a premium along the North Pier. Each pleasure boat had an allocated berth as well as permission to display notice

board(s) on the pier to advertise sailings. Adverts were also placed in newspapers and holiday guides, the newspaper advert for *Thornwick's* weekly sailings for the 10th – 17th September 1949 shows a very comprehensive programme at 4/- (20p) a head and a special request cruise to Whitby at 10/- (50p). If all the boats were along the pier at the same time it could become very crowded indeed and at the Harbour Masters discretion the South pier could, and often was, used to relieve congestion.

At the end of her 1949 summer season *Yorkshireman*, although more use to river work in the Humber, was pressed into use with sister tugs *Krooman, Brahman* and *Airman* to help bring the tanker *Borren Hill*, stranded on the Sherringham Shoal, into the Humber.

9
The 1950's and 60's

The Heyday of the Pleasure Boats

Bridlington entered the 1950's with the post war pleasure boat trade at an all time high and her five home based pleasure boats, *Britannia, Boys' Own, Bridlington Queen, Yorkshire Belle,* and *Thornwick* together with the *Yorkshireman* were as popular as ever. Cheap air travel and foreign holidays had yet to take effect so there were plenty of holiday visitors to Bridlington. The basing of *Yorkshireman* at Bridlington provided much needed revenue for the harbour authorities, between 1948 and 1951 her owners, the United Towing Co., paid Bridlington Harbour Commissioners £2623 19s 6d to cover harbour dues and all charges including entry dues, water, phone and notice boards. The end of petrol rationing in May 1950 meant that the boatmen no longer had to worry about having a sufficient petrol allocation to meet seasonal demand, it also resulted in more use of coaches and cars for pleasure purposes although the train was still the most popular means of holiday travel. Although the number of holidaymakers, particularly day trippers, continued to increase, the peak holiday periods of Whitsun, Easter and the August Bank Holiday were very dependent on the weather with the larger pleasure boats with covered accommodation being preferred over the 'open' boats like *Britannia* and the cobles.

(Authors Collection)

Bridlington Harbour in the 1950's
(left to right) Coble *Liberty,* pleasure boats *Britannia* and *Bridlington Queen*

The aging *Britannia,* now in her thirties needed updating to compete successfully with the other pleasure boats and at some time in the 1950's she was substantially rebuilt, probably re-engined, and her appearance changed dramatically from that of her pre-war days. She now had an elevated covered wheelhouse with a large framework extending from the wheelhouse almost to the square stern. A protective awning was fitted which could be rolled out over the framework for the comfort and protection of those passengers seated underneath. Gloria Taylor, of Haisthorpe, remembers in the 1950s when she was about 18 or 20 spending a lot of time with her father George 'Young Brannie' Welburn, on the *Britannia*. On one sunny occasion she was wearing only a swim suit when the engine back-fired near the sand bank. The shock made her fall overboard and she had to be retrieved by her father using a long pole with a hook on the end of it.

On the 12th March 1951 after nearly four years of operation *Yorkshire Belle* returned to CWG for modifications and the replacement of her Crossley diesel engines with twin Gardiner 8 cylinder 152 bhp diesel engines. The work was completed by the 27th April and she returned to Bridlington.

The old problem of carrying too many passengers arose again in July 1952 when the Skipper, as master, of the *Bridlington Queen* pleaded guilty to carrying excess passengers, i.e. 160 passengers instead of the 144 passengers plus six crew that the *Bridlington Queen* was permitted to carry.

(Bridlington Library)

Bridlington Queen with closed bridge and hull rubbing strip added

Passengers disembarking had been checked off it by the senior nautical officer of the Ministry of Transport, and the Bridlington Corporation boating inspector and surveyor of ships for the ministry, who recorded on a hand-clock 160 aboard, 16 more passengers than the legal loading. Bridlington magistrate ordered the Skipper to pay a £15 fine and costs of £6/2/0d. For the owner of *Bridlington Queen*, Robert Ingram, who pleaded guilty to permitting the offence, his legal representative submitted that as the magistrates had found the Skipper guilty, there was no case for his client to answer as the law read "master or owner". The chairman upheld the defence and announced that, after careful consideration, the magistrates were of the opinion that if the law had meant both master and owner to be held responsible it would have said so.

Another couple of 'incidents' in 1952 saw a number of holidaymakers disembarking from the pleasure boat *Britannia* tipped into the harbour at low tide when a gangplank resting between the boat and the landing stage overturned. Boatmen and fishermen rushed to pull them out and it was fortunate that there was little water in the harbour or the situation could have been more serious. The second 'incident' was to an engineer on the *Boys' Own,* who suffered a severely lacerated hand when a rope he threw to boatmen on the pier fouled the boats propeller, tightened and trapped his hand against the side of the vessel.

In October that year a joint scheme between British Railways and Bridlington Corporation saw a poster designed by the famous artist Frank A. A. Wootton to promote rail travel to the Yorkshire coastal resort of Bridlington. Produced for British Railways (BR), North Eastern Region (NER) the poster was displayed at various stations during 1953 and 1954 and shows the pleasure boat *Yorkshire Belle* full of holidaymakers and surrounded by seagulls, approaching the harbour entrance.

One of the tourist attractions In the early 1950's that would be frowned on today was watching the Flamborough egg "climmers" at work.

(Arthur Newby)

Skipper Walter Newby takes *Bridlington Queen* along the base of Flamborough cliffs

"Climming" involved lowering men over the edge of the cliffs to collect eggs from nesting sea birds as a method of supplementing incomes. The practice of "Climming" is believed to have started about 1900 and comprised four men in an egg gathering gang, one suspended by the rope, who climbed down to collect the eggs, signaling by a hand line and using his feet to keep himself from the cliff face (similar to the abseiling of today) and three at the top. It was on these three men, and the strength of the rope, that the climber depended. Of course the rope was carefully examined each time, but the cliff's razor sharp flints could fray it, and lumps of loose chalk or flint, knocked out of place by startled birds, could fall and hit the climber, so that most of them wore thick head coverings or caps stuffed with straw and their Gansey's as added protection against the elements. Three to four-hundred eggs could be collected in a day and sold to locals and visitors' Guillemot eggs, which are large for the size of bird, were particularly sought after. One way to sell their eggs was to abseil down the rope on to the decks of pleasure boats and sell the eggs to the passengers as shown in the picture of *Bridlington Queen* at the base of the cliffs where the "climmers" would be working. Despite the danger, few accidents were recorded and "egg climming" continued until 1954 when it was finally made illegal.

The pleasure tug *Yorkshireman* had returned to the Humber after another successful 1952 season, when the greatest storm surge on record for the North Sea occurred on 31 January - 1 February 1953. The surge height reyyached 9 feet (2.74m) at Southend in Essex, 9.7 feet (2.97m) at King's Lynn in Norfolk and 11 feet (3.36m) in the Netherlands. The shingle spit of Spurn Head in Yorkshire was breached. Soon after darkness fell, Lincolnshire bore the brunt of the storm. Sand was scoured from beaches and sand hills, timber-piled dunes were breached, the landward slopes of embankments were eroded, concrete sea walls crumbled, the promenades of Mablethorpe and Sutton-on-Sea were wrecked, and seawater broke through to flood agricultural land. Although Bridlington escaped the worst of the storm, boats were damaged in the harbour, the North and South piers were awash and the Chicken Run Jetty submerged. The *Yorkshireman* acted as a communications centre at sea, maintaining radio contact between vessels needing assistance and the tugs going to their aid. *Yorkshireman's* attributes as a tug also proved useful in June 1953 when she was used to tow a whale out to sea. The 35 foot (10.6m) long bull-nosed whale weighed 40 tons and had become stranded on Bridlington's south beach. A ferry boat was used to hitch one end of a 720 foot (219m) long 6 inch (152mm) diameter manila rope around the tail of the whale and take the other end to the *Yorkshireman*.

Throughout the 1950's the holidaymakers booking a holiday at Bridlington rose steadily and given good weather their numbers were increased by the day trippers. Special excursion trains were added, coach and car parks were full as were the hotels and boarding houses. The harbour boatmen did good business as for many holidaymakers no visit to Bridlington was complete without a walk around the harbour and a 'sail' on one or more of the pleasure boats. The smaller ships of the Royal Navy often made Courtesy visits and would anchor in Bridlington Bay. The boatmen were not slow to take advantage of this by adding 'trips around the warship' to their itineraries.

The early 1950"s saw further changes of ownership when the well known fisherman and coble owner Alf Wright together with two business partners acquired the pleasure boat *Britannia* from Robert Ingram. In August 1954 they also acquired the *Bridlington Queen* from Robert Ingram and formed the Bridlington Queen Company Limited to own and operate her, Alf Wright then became her skipper. These two changes of ownership are believed to have marked the end of Robert Ingram's involvement in Bridlington pleasure boats.

Many of the pleasure boats finished their summer sailing programmes in September and *Thornwick* was no exception, under the command of Captain C. G. Broughton CBE, she made her end of season sail on the 15th September 1954 with a special cruise to Whitby for an adult fare of 10 shillings (50p), children half price.

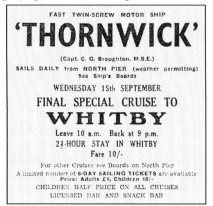

End of season 'Final Cruise' poster for *Thornwick*

1955 was a mixed year for Bridlington with a record Easter with crowds of people on the North Pier many of whom enjoyed a trip on the pleasure boats in the harbour. A Whitsun marred by a rail strike and coal shortages and an August that saw over 41,000 visitors by rail alone.

Despite the large number of holiday makers taking trips on the pleasure boats, United Towing Co., owners of *Yorkshireman*, decided to finish their pleasure steamer activities and at the end of her 1955 summer season she left Bridlington to work full time as a jetty tug in the Humber. She had been based at Bridlington for every summer season from 1928 to 1939 and from 1947 to 1955, a grand total of 19 years. Her subsequent history is detailed in appendix 4.

The educational benefits of the pleasure boats was not ignored and in June 1956 thirty two pupils from Burlington (Bridlington) Junior School took a trip to Whitby on the *Thornwick*. They had prepared for the trip by studying books, maps and charts. While onboard the *Thornwick*, various navigational aids and places of interest were pointed out to them, but the trip was remembered by one former pupil with the words "many of the children were seasick".

The Bridlington boating community lost a well known member with the sudden death of Albert Hutchinson in October 1956 at the age of 61. Albert had been connected with the sea all his life and at the time of his death was one of the co-owners of the pleasure boats *Britannia* and *Bridlington Queen*.

Congestion in the harbour was still a problem particularly at low tide; this was made worst when events such as the Sea Angling Festival in September forced the boats into competing for the same depth of water. The pleasure boats and angling cobles would all be bunched up near the harbour entrance with more anglers in ferry boats waiting to be ferried out to more cobles waiting in the Bay. It may have been congestion that caused *Thornwick* to be in the news again on the 7th September 1957 when she collided with the end of the harbour Jetty.

During this period *Boys' Own* was, tides permitting, operating a full sailing program with a pre-breakfast trip, three or four day time trips followed by an after tea and an evening trip. Musical entertainment was provided on board by the well known accordionist Bobby Fisher. Touting for business on the North pier (known as spawning) was an important part of the shore crews duties and William 'Rosy' Rose, a Norfolk man, would shout "Sailing now on Boys' Own, leaving right away, ladies lavatory on board".

Boys' Own , like many other pleasure boats, had several experienced local boatmen and fishermen who were capable 'skippers' and could take charge of the boat and it's passengers and crew when required. They included David 'Boyzie' Crawford, George Johnson and Richard 'Dick' Crawford. Over time members of the 'skippers' families also served as crew members including David Crawford's son also named David, and George Johnson's brother, Frank 'Kel' Johnson. George Johnson's son George was also a crew member along with his dog 'Whisky' who had a knitted jumper with *Boys' Own* on it just like the rest of the crew.

(Mike Milner)

The Crew of the Boys Own about 1958
(Left to right) George Johnson, Frank 'Kel' Johnson, Dick Crawford, Stan Milner, Fred Milner, George 'Geordie' Adamson, Lt. Edward Taylor (Bridlington Harbourmaster), William 'Rosy' Rose.
(The lady in front has not been identified).

Part owner and crewman Fred Milner had a son named Eric who was a founding member of the Bridlington Sub Aqua Club. On many occasions he was called upon to free the propellers of ropes etc picked up by the boat in the harbour mouth at low tide.

Mooring space within the harbour was relieved to some extent in October 1958 with the closing down of 1104 Marine Craft Unit of the RAF and the transfer of its three launches (pinnaces) to Calshot. By May 1959, even with *Yorkshireman* gone, the Bridlington Harbour Master was reporting that the harbour was overcrowded with many boats being berthed six abreast. Berths were needed for 16 keelboats, 22 large cobles, 24 small cobles, 64 cabin cruisers, 35 yachts, 12 dinghies (sail and power), 11 private rowing boats, 87 commercial rowing boats, 20 ferry boats, 4 speedboats and five pleasure boats. *Britannia, Boys' Own, Bridlington Queen, Yorkshire Belle,* and *Thornwick* Any relief on mooring space released by the Marine Craft Unit was short lived as in May 1959 Bridlington Corporation received notification that the unit would be re-established later that year.

(Authors Collection)

A busy Bridlington Harbour about 1959 with *Bridlington Queen, Boys' Own and Thornwick,*
the two large launches/speedboats *Blue Bird* and *Swift* are to the right.

The 1960 season started well for the boatmen, with *Bridlington Queen* and *Yorkshire Belle* arriving in April from their winter lay-up – a sure sign that the holidays were about to start. Easter was better than the previous year and Whitson was jam-packed with an estimated 100,000 holidaymakers arriving over the weekend. People on the pleasure boats in August were treated to the sight of a freak storm in which lightning, thunder, torrential rain and snow hit Bridlington. However the most significant event of the year for the pleasure boat owners was when the consortium that owned *Boys' Own* sold her to Trevor Silverwood of Flamborough for £10,000 and Trevor became the sole owner.

A pointer to the future came the next year when following poor weather at Easter and Whitsun the number of holiday makers making 'weekly' or 'fortnight' bookings for August were overtaken for the first time by the number wanting 'week end only' accommodation. A worrying trend for the boatmen who relied heavily on attracting passengers every day in the summer to return a decent profit as operating costs, safety related costs, boat maintenance costs, license and harbour dues etc. were all increasing As if to prove the weather cynics wrong Bridlington had a 'Golden Egg Easter' the following year with over 9,000 visitors by rail alone. July was also good and led to the master of *Yorkshire Belle*, appearing before Bridlington Magistrates Court charged with carrying too many passengers. Philip R. Marshall, prosecuting on behalf of the Ministry of Transport said the *Yorkshire Belle* was authorized to carry 222 passengers plus a crew of five. On 21 July 1963 a nautical surveyor from Hull was on duly at Bridlington at 4.15 p.m. when the *Yorkshire Belle* returned from an excursion. He and a marine surveyor assistant counted the passengers as they came ashore, and the total was 243, an excess of 21. On 31 July the passengers were checked as they came off the *Yorkshire Belle* from another cruise. On that occasion there were 233 on board, an excess of 11. The master pleaded guilty to the two charges and was fined £25 plus five Guineas advocate's fee.

The pattern of unsettled weather together with more people coming 'on spec' made it very difficult to predict how many holidaymakers would arrive and as a consequence how many of those would want to go on the Pleasure Boats. In general Bridlington was fortunate that for a good percentage of the holidaymakers their holiday was incomplete without one or more trips in the bay or a longer cruise to Scarborough or Whitby. The August Bank Holiday in 1963 and the Whitsuntide Holiday in 1964 are just two examples of the boatmen's dilemma, The 1963 August Bank Holiday was the dreariest and quietest bank holiday on record, appalling weather throughout the weekend kept thousands of people away from the seaside. People who had booked for a, week or a fortnight came as usual, but practically no-one came looking for accommodation for the three days of the weekend. The cause or all this was a spell of weather that brought no sunshine throughout Saturday, Sunday or Monday, with a fine drizzle for most of the weekend and nearly an inch and a half of rain on Sunday. Altogether it was a sad weekend which cost the boatmen and the town thousands of pounds in lost revenue. The 1964 \Whitsuntide holiday by comparison was wonderful as the temperatures shot into the sixties on Saturday and Sunday. Cars and motor-cycles came in their thousands, plus 302 coaches. A total of 25,200 arrived by train, there were 23 excursion trains on Monday and they were all full, with 10 of them 'bursting at the seams'. The Boatmen and other Tradesmen did well, the holiday break giving them a tremendous boost and as an added benefit the good weather and the influx of holidaymakers continued throughout the week. Unfortunately the master of *Yorkshire Belle* appeared again before Bridlington Magistrates Court charged with carrying too many passengers. Philip R. Marshall, for the Ministry of Transport, said that the master had carried an excess of 20 passengers on 25 August and on the following day 4 passengers too many. He was found guilty and ordered to pay 3 pounds and 3 shillings costs and 5 shillings for each passenger over the maximum allowed.

The Ministry of Transport regarded the overloading of pleasure vessels very seriously, as the life-saving apparatus onboard is based on the number of passengers carried. However the counting of passengers was not as straightforward as it sounds. Counting was recorded on a hand held counter, the number allowed on board was the number on the license plus the crew but not counting children under one year old. At peak periods with holidaymakers milling around the pier and gangplank, some children being carried aboard as 'free' others 'toddling' on and off, friends jostling back and forth to stay together as a group all made accurate counting difficult. There was always the possibility of being interrupted while counting and it was even more difficult if two boats were moored alongside each other, as frequently happened, and passengers crossed from one boat to the other, there was always a remote chance that some people had remained on board from a previous voyage. These were just some of the factors that made the process subject to error. All of this was usually irrelevant to the court unless the master of the boat had strong supporting evidence in his favour. It was significant that there was never any evidence or charge of reckless loading. The pleasure boats were sailed by local fishermen who knew every .square yard of the sea in Bridlington Bay and beyond and there was little possibility of anybody being in danger.

10
The Slow Decline of the Pleasure Boats

Britannia, Bridlington Queen and *Thornwick* leave
and *Boys' Own* becomes *Flamborian*

Although Bridlington was still a popular holiday destination in the 1960s, cheap air travel made holidays abroad more attractive and UK resorts began to see a slow reduction in the number of visitors. Fred Pontin had opened Pontinental centers on the Mediterranean Coast in 1963 and could offer a 14 day all inclusive holiday with guaranteed sunshine for £50. The choice of foreign holiday destinations and the mobility offered by car ownership meant that the annual holiday was no longer automatically a week or fortnight at the same seaside resort year after year. Consequently U.K. seaside resorts saw a decline in the long stay holidaymakers in favour of relatively 'low-spend' visitors and day trippers. This decline in numbers became particularly apparent from the mid 1960's onwards. The Easter holiday in 1965 proved to be bleak and the Bridlington boatmen were saddened to hear of the death of David Crawford who had been captain of the pleasure boat *Boys' Own* for 10 years in the 1940's and 1950's.

On a warm Saturday evening in the summer of 1965, the pleasure-boat *Bridlington Queen* raced across Bridlington Bay with 90 passengers on board to rescue four people whose outboard motor-boat had capsized. The pleasure boat was about to tie-up in the Harbour when the crew were told that three adults and a child had been seen clinging to an up-turned boat about a mile off Sewerby. None of the passengers were in a hurry to get off so the boat immediately turned round and went to help. Lifebelts were thrown from the *Bridlington Queen* to the four in the water and then they were hauled on board and their boat was towed back to the Harbour. Those rescued were Peter Burton, the works manager of the Burton Engineering Company at Bridlington, his eight-year-old son, Nicholas and his sister-in-law and nephew Mrs. L. Held and Mr. D. Reid, both of Blackpool. Mr. Burton told a local reporter

> "We launched the boat from the North Beach jetty, and were planning to
> do some fishing, the sea was quite calm, but we got into a cross-current
> and the boat fell into a trough and overturned. No one panicked and we
> just clung to the upturned boat until help arrived".

Although the August holiday started with better weather, a force 8 gale was experienced by the end of August which caused the *Thornwick* to turn back to Bridlington while passing Flamborough Head on the first stage of her Journey to Scarborough. The gale force winds also hit the 3,000-ton oil drilling rig Endeavour which was being maneuvered by two tugs into position 13 miles off Scarborough when the wind snapped the 1½ inch (38 mm) diameter towing cables and set her adrift. It was not until the rig had drifted along the coast to Flamborough Head that the tugs *Utrecht* and *Nordholm* managed to take it in tow again and after an all-day wait to haul the rig back on station, efforts were abandoned and it was decided to park it in Bridlington Bay about 4 miles from Bridlington harbour and 3 miles off Barmston where its three 190 foot (58 metre) legs were lowered onto the sea bed while repairs were carried out. Bridlington boatmen were quick to realise the rig's potential as a holiday attraction and business began to boom as hundreds of holiday makers queued each day for trips round the rig. Fares which began at 2/6p (12½.p) soon rose to 4/- (20p) a head for the 70 minute cruises, which included close-up views of the £3m structure.

Shuttle services to the rig and back ran from breakfast time to dusk, and when the tide was out ferry boats were used to carry passengers to the pleasure-boats anchored off the Beach.

(The Bayle Museum)

Bridlington Queen operating off the beach

But while the money rolled into the pockets of local boatmen, the rig's American owners, Signal Oil and Gas Company, were losing £6.000 a day in wasted time, operating costs, and depreciation. On the shore, visitors queued for a one minute close-up view of the rig through the 'penny-in-the-slot' telescopes and souvenir postcard-size photographs of it were being sold at 1/6 (7.5p) each.

The slow decline in the number of holiday visitors was making it impossible to economically sustain the aging *Britannia* and the four larger pleasure boats, *Boys' Own, Bridlington Queen, Yorkshire Belle,* and *Thornwick.* At the end of the 1965 season *Thornwick,* which ironically at 17 years old was the youngest pleasure boat, is believed to have ceased operating from Bridlington and was subsequently purchased by Croson Ltd and the Bournemouth, Swanage and Poole Steam Packet Company (trading as the Dorset Belles) to replace the paddle steamer *Embassy* on their Isle of Wight services, the subsequent history of *Thornwick* is detailed in appendix 4

(Bridlington Library)

Thornwick in her final 'all white' colour scheme

At the start of the 1966 season, Bridlington was down to three large pleasure boats, *Boys' Own, Bridlington Queen* and *Yorkshire Belle* and the old motor boat *Britannia*. The busiest, sunniest dream Whitsun occurred at the end of May in 1966 when Bridlington had the sort of weather holidaymakers dream about and traders hope for but rarely see. Hour after hour of sunshine over the weekend saw more than 12,000 cars stream into the town and many more holiday makers arriving by train. The beaches and the harbour were crowded and the pleasure boats did a roaring trade. Several passengers on the pleasure-boat *Boys' Own* were thrown onto the deck when it hit a sandbank while leaving Bridlington Harbour on Tuesday morning; three of them received cuts and bruises. Trevor Silverwood, .skipper of the vessel, said

> "A sandbank has built up at the Harbour mouth during the winter and we
> caught it as we were leaving the Harbour".

The sandbank was the notorious 'Canch', a 300 yard long sandbar outside the harbour which claimed a second victim on Sunday the 17th July 1966. The pleasure-steamer *Bridlington Queen*, with more than 110 holiday makers on board, had just started her first pleasure cruise that morning when she struck a submerged rock on the Canch and quickly began to settle by the stern. Arthur Jenkinson, one of the owners of the speed-boat *007* was in the Harbour when the alarm was given. He went out to the *Bridlington Queen* to see what was happening. When he found the pleasure-boat was sinking he returned to the Harbour and towed out a string of ferryboats. By now a flotilla of rescue boats, ferryboats, rowing-boats, and speedboats, had come to her aid.

(Bridlington Library)

Bridlington Queen sinking with *Yorkshire Belle* standing by

There was no panic among the passengers and they calmly stepped down into the rescue boats which were towed back to harbour by the speedboats. All the passengers, including a group of Norwegian exchange pupils on their first full day in Bridlington, arrived back on dry land without getting their feet wet. One of the passengers, said

"We had just left the harbour when we felt a jolt, the boat went on a bit and then started going astern, she then started taking in water and the ferry boats were called out to take off the passengers. The stern was well down by the time we were taken off and the seat cushions were floating."

The *Bridlington Queen* sank further until the stem was on the bottom in about five feet (1.5 metres) of water. In fact, she would probably have remained partially afloat had she not settled on the bottom first, because, like other sea-going pleasure cruisers, her hull was divided by bulkheads into separate compartments. Ken Ward, Dennis Gough and Robin Broadley, members of the East Yorkshire Sub-Aqua Club went beneath the *Bridlington Queen* to inspect the damage. The propellers were intact but there was a 2 foot by 1 foot (0.6 by 0.3 metre) hole near the keel. The hole was plugged with cushions and cloths which enabled the pumps brought aboard by Bridlington firemen to begin taking the water out and refloat the vessel. When the *Bridlington Queen* was afloat she was towed back into Bridlington Harbour by the pleasure boat *Boys' Own*.

(Bridlington Library)

Boys' Own preparing to take the tow

The pumping operation went on for 10 hours until in the afternoon at low tide the water started to run out of the hole and proper repairs could be undertaken. On Monday, members of the sub aqua club marked the position of the rock, which was in the middle of the main shipping channel through the Canch, and a fishing trawler towed it off to deeper water. It was said at the time that some of the larger boats had been operating with only a few inches clearance above the rock, however it now seems that the rock was snagged by a trawler the day before, it was lifted but broke free and dropped back in the sea just as the trawler was over the Canch. *Bridlington Queen* was quickly repaired and rejoined *Boys' Own* and *Yorkshire Belle* sailing from the harbour.

During 1966, at the request of the owners of the three remaining large pleasure boats, the Council Foreshore Committee proposed an increase in pleasure boat charges from 2/6p (12½.p) to 3/- (15p) per trip for trips up to 45 minutes and from 5/- (25p) to 6/- (30p) per trip for trips of 1½ hours. The proposal was accepted and Bridlington Council passed a bye law increasing the amount they could charge for pleasure trips.

The *Bridlington Queen* was in the news again in September when a message was received that an Enterprise-class dinghy had overturned off Fraisthorpe and that the two man crew appeared to be in difficulties. The *Bridlington Queen* immediately went to their assistance and had one man on board when an air sea rescue helicopter from R.A.F

Leconfield arrived and picked up the other member of the crew. The dinghy was towed back to Bridlington Harbour behind the *Bridlington Queen.*

The increased charges for pleasure trips were monitored by the boating inspector and in July 1967 the skipper of the Yorkshire Belle, was fined £5 for charging a higher fare than he was entitled to. This came about when the pleasure boats were running one hour trips at 4/- (20p) around the pirate radio station 270, on MV *Oceaan VII*, anchored in international waters off Bridlington and owned by Ellambar Investments Ltd. of Scarborough. The boating inspector timed two of the Yorkshire Belle trips as lasting only 45 minutes. In fairness to the skipper it was stated that no passengers had complained.

The old problem of harbour space was again raised in January 1968 when due to a 200% increase in the fishing fleet, from 12 keelboats to 32 keelboats over five years, the harbour master, Captain Roly Spears, reported that the harbour was at full capacity and causing a growing problem of berthing space.

On Friday 31st May 1968 *Boys' Own* returned to the harbour with a new shape and a new name, *Flamborian.*

(Authors Collection)

Flamborian in Bridlington Harbour in the early 1970's

She had been extensively altered over the winter months by Hepworths at their boatyard at Paull on the Humber. Her ships boat and davits had been removed and replaced by modern life rafts, the tubular structure and its canvas awning had also gone. Her sides and top had been filled in with a new superstructure which extended aft almost to the stern and had seven large window cut outs each side. Her bridge roof had been widened to cover the full width of the boat and passenger seating was provided on top of and inside the extended superstructure. Her twin Kelvin engines had been replaced by twin Gardner 6LXs rated at 116hp each which consumed about six gallons (27.3 litres) per hour when cruising. Her passenger seating space had been increased but without altering her carrying capacity of 180, though this was later reduced in line with more cautious regulations that were introduced in the 1990s following the Marchioness disaster on the River Thames. She was fitted with toilets, a saloon bar, a separate ladies cabin aft and a very stylish new funnel.

Flamborian arrived back in the harbour in time for the 1968 Whit week-end which again proved to be a record one with excellent weather and thousands of visitors. 4,800 arrived by train on Saturday including three private trains bringing members of working men's clubs. Sunday was busier with fifteen trains bringing an estimated 6,000 holiday makers from Hull, Beverley, Leeds, Huddersfield, Wakefield and one special train from Chesterfield and Grantham. On Monday fifteen additional trains arrived at Bridlington station bringing an estimated 8,000 people. Many more holiday makers arrived over the weekend by coach or car. There were 14,000 cars and 190 coaches parked on the Corporation car parks. Over 33,000 deckchairs were hired out and many of the holidaymakers 'took to the water' with pleasure cruises on the *Britannia, Flamborian, Bridlington Queen* and *Yorkshire Belle*. Impressive though the Bank Holiday visitor figures may seem, they are not a reliable guide as they fluctuate widely over the years according to the weather and those of 1968 masked the general falling off in visitor numbers for all UK holiday resorts.

In August 1968 the *Bridlington Queen* was purchased by Desmond Connelly of Bridlington from her operating company, Bridlington Queen Ltd., which was then wound up. The crew was retained and the skipper was George Welburn, a former coxswain of the Bridlington lifeboat. About this time *Britannia,* despite extensive rework over the years, ceased working as a pleasure boat though she remained at Bridlington in a new role as an angling launch.

Councillor Trevor Silverwood, skipper and owner of the pleasure-boat *Flamborian,* announced in May 1969 that

> "The owners of Bridlington's three pleasure boats, *Bridlington Queen, Flamborian* and *Yorkshire Belle,* will not be competing with one another for passengers this season".

The pleasure-boat owners had devised a scheme to work together this year to give the holidaymakers better value for money. In the past, passengers had to wait on board until each boat had a full load for a trip to sea with all three boats competing against each other on the piers to get passengers on 'their' boat. Under the new system the boats will be filled one by one and the profits would be shared proportionately between the three boat owners with all the passengers' takings going to one pay-box. Desmond Connelly owner of the *Bridlington Queen* added

> "This will enable us to provide a better variety of sea trips for holidaymakers, For example, we intend to run trips to areas where skin divers will be working on wrecks in the Bridlington area."

The question of dredging safe channels through the Canch sandbar arose again in June 1969 after the *Flamborian* grounded and was stuck for 3½ hours. Her 65 passengers were taken off by ferryboats and *Flamborian* floated off later at high tide. The pleasure boat owners were concerned that if the Canch was not regularly dredged they would lose thousands of pounds in revenue due to restrictions in the times for safe passage out of and into the harbour. At this time the Harbour Commissioners did not own a dredger but used the *Esk* from Whitby as and when a dredger was needed.

In August passengers on the *Bridlington Queen* skippered by George Welburn saw dozens of basking sharks off Bridlington. In September ownership of *Yorkshire Belle* passed to John Cross (Jack) Pockley and Thomas Marshall Neeham of Bridlington. October saw the highest tide for 16 years flood the harbour and adjacent shops. The high tide was whipped up by the wind with the moored boats riding high above the piers. The pleasure boat *Flamborian* was level with the Chicken Run Jetty which was flooded over and Harbour Road was under four feet (1.2m) of water. Fortunately there was no damage to the boats when the water subsided.

The 1970's were very mixed for the boatmen with typical boom and gloom weather. The local bye-laws were amended to allow an increase in passenger fees from 4 shillings (20p) to 5 shillings (25p) max per hour. In July 1970 a passenger on the *Yorkshire Belle* alerted the skipper Jack Pockley to a capsized dingy, Jim Havercroft, accordionist on the *Yorkshire Belle* dived in and rescued one man, the speedboat *007* rescued two more but a fourth man was lost.

The pleasure boat *Flamborian* temporarily left Bridlington on the 20 February 1972 for Hull, to maintain the Hull to New Holland ferry service run by British Rail. The service was usually run by two of British Rail Ferry Service's three paddle steamers *Tattershall Castle*, *Lincoln Castle* and *Wingfield Castle*. All three were coal burners and the miners strike had resulted in insufficient coal stocks to maintain the service. One of the paddle steamers was undergoing maintenance and the other was laid up at the start of the strike on the 9 January. The remaining paddle steamer was *Tattershall Castle* and she was expected to run out of coal by the time *Flamborian* arrived. *Flamborian* would operate a 'passenger only' service so all vehicular traffic would have to make a long detour via Boothferry Bridge. In the event *Flamborian* did not stay long in her new role as the strike ended on the 25 February and as soon as coal stocks were replenished *Flamborian* returned to Bridlington.

In a surprise move in April 1972 Trevor Silverwood sold *Flamborian* to Desmond Connelly who also owned the pleasure boat *Bridlington Queen*. Unfortunately the new master of the *Flamborian* appeared before Bridlington Magistrates Court in September charged with carrying too many passengers on Whit Monday. H. A. Haines, for the Ministry of Transport, said that Captain Gunnill, an inspector for the Department, had carried out a check and counted 186 passengers - six more than the license allowed. Desmond Connelly was found not guilty and his well presented defense was based on the complex rules about children and his method of ensuring that passengers were counted properly. His method was for one crewman to take tickets at the entrance to the gangplank with another next to him with a counter and a third crew member at the bottom with another counter. They counted every passenger regardless of age and as an added precaution they started the counters at two and checked the boat after every voyage for any 'stowaways'. A further discrepancy in the prosecutions evidence was that Captain Gunnill saw no children he thought were under one and did not see any prams on board yet members of the crew stated that as it was Whit Monday the boat was full of families with about sixty children of various ages and about a dozen prams – the case was dismissed.

At the end of the 1973 season *Yorkshire Belle* changed hands again and became the property of J. T. Bogg, Arthur Strike Cook and J. F. Bogg, all of Bridlington. She was to be operated by Bogg Holdings Group on behalf of her owners.

Britannia, although no longer a pleasure boat, was taken to Scarborough in April 1974 to have a new keel and stabilizer fins (bilge keels) fitted by Scarborough Marine Engineers. About this time her engines were replaced by twin Perkins 4236 diesels. When the work was completed she returned to Bridlington to continue her role as an angling launch.

The three pleasure boats, *Bridlington Queen, Flamborian* and *Yorkshire Belle,* continued to work together and were advertised as 'Bridlington Pleasure Steamers' offering a wide range of pleasure trips. Long trips every morning round the caves to view the famous seabird sanctuary at Bempton and then out to the shipping lanes. Shorter one hour trips to Flamborough Head, viewing the historic Danes Dyke and other interesting landmarks. All vessels were stated to be fully equipped to the highest Board of Trade standards and ticket could be purchased at the pay booth on the North Pier and advance party reservations could be made by telephone.

The problems associated with grounding on the Canch were largely resolved when Bridlington Harbour Commissioners (B.H.C.) acquired their own grab dredger. She arrived as *Essex Lady* during the first week of February 1978 and had been found on the river Esk in Whitby where she had been left following wreck salvage work. She had a very interesting history herself being built in 1940 by Lobnitz & Co. Ltd. of Renfrew Scotland as yard No. 794, one of fifteen 'Sandchime' class steam powered dredgers. She was named *Prittlewell* and it is believed that she spent the war years keeping the channels to the Thames Forts clear. After the war she worked for Southend-on-Sea County Borough and in 1971 was bought by Essex County Council who renamed her *Essex Lady* and converted her to a gravel barge with a Ruston diesel engine. After being purchased by B.H.C. she had an extensive refit in the dry dock at Hull during which she was extensively modernised, converted back to a grab dredger with a new crane and her Ruston engine replaced by a Volvo engine. Shortly after her arrival in Bridlington she was renamed *Gypsy Race* after the stream that rises in the Wolds, enters the north-west corner of the harbour by Clough Hole and is responsible for bringing most of the mud which has to be regularly dredged out of the harbour. Her name being chosen by the B.H.C. after a competition to name her held among school children in the Bridlington Area. She is currently Certificate number: 460 in the historic register of ships.

About 1977 the Bogg Holdings Group, operators of *Yorkshire Belle* and British Rail Sealink entered into an agreement to have the *Yorkshire Belle* on stand-by for the Humber Ferry Service. The three paddle steamers that usually operated the service were now down to one. *Tattershall Castle* had been withdrawn in 1972 and *Wingfield Castle* in 1974, leaving *Lincoln Castle* as the sole survivor. To maintain a two ship service British Rail had transferred their Isle of Wight ferry *Farringford* to work alongside the *Lincoln Castle* but if anyone of them required maintenance there was no further cover, hence the agreement with Bogg Holdings Group.

In June 1979, despite Bridlington Harbour Commissioners having their own dredger, all three pleasure boats ground on the Canch when they returned from their last trips of the day at about 5.30 pm. They were stuck for just over one hour until they all refloated on the incoming tide and arrived back into Bridlington Harbour after 6.30pm. There was no damage to the pleasure boats and no passengers were injured although many were day trippers and missed their scheduled coaches and trains and had to make their own way home.

On the evening of Sunday 15th July 1979 *Bridlington Queen* grounded on a concrete block in Bridlington harbour at low tide and began taking in water. The boat, one of two owned by Councillor Des Connelly – the other being *Flamborian,* was moored alongside the Chicken Run jetty after completing her day's work when Councillor Connelly received a call that she was 'sinking'. Bridlington fire service was called out and the firemen spent about an hour and a half pumping out the pleasure boat.

(Bayle Museum)

Bridlington Queen by the North Pier.

Although described by the press as 'sinking', being low tide she had simply settled on the bottom with one of her hull compartments breached by the concrete block. After the water had been pumped out a temporary repair was made and on Monday *Bridlington Queen* was taken to a dry dock at Grimsby where permanent repairs were carried out.

Bridlington nearly gained a fourth pleasure boat, albeit a static one, when in July 1979 an informal application was received from Shepherd Wood Studios for a berth in Bridlington Harbour for the former Humber Ferry *Wingfield Castle*, currently berthed In King George V Docks, London. A formal application was not proceeded with and the proposal lapsed. Pressure on space from fishing vessels in the harbour would have been one drawback and the fact that she would have to have her paddle wheels removed to get through the harbour entrance was another, the suggestion that she could be moored outside the harbour was impractical.

One call for *Yorkshire Belle* to operate the Humber Ferry came in early October 1979 after the *Farrlngford* had to be withdrawn for emergency structural repairs after being damaged when it struck a pier head. There was no other back up, the *Lincoln Castle* had failed a boiler inspection in 1978 and had been withdraw as uneconomical to repair because the ferry service was scheduled for closure when the Humber Bridge opened in 1981. *Yorkshire Belle* operated a 'foot passengers only' ferry service over the weekend until the *Farrlngford* returned to service. Fortunately the back up call came out of season but it could have been at any time during the summer.

At the end of 1979, Yorkshire and Humberside were managing to attract seven per cent of all the people who took a holiday in Britain, only the West Country (20%), South (10%) South East and East Anglia (8% each) were attracting more people. While there was an increasing number taking their main holiday abroad there had been quite a considerable increase in people taking second, or even third or fourth holidays and day trips within their own country. Guesthouses and small hotels now provided only 10% of holiday accommodation, with an increasing number of people using a caravan or taking a holiday flat. More people were staying with friends or relatives for second holidays. This growth in the domestic holiday market, in a period of slow economic growth was most welcome to the Bridlington boat owners who had managed to successfully run three large pleasure boats throughout the 1970's. Unfortunately any growth came too late for the aging *Britannia,* although no longer a pleasure boat, she left Bridlington in 1979 after being sold by her owner Mike Tranmer to Tom Furey of Ireland. Her career at Bridlington as a pleasure boat and angling launch had been a long one and had lasted for 56 years. Her subsequent history is detailed in appendix 4.

Although the Yorkshire Belle had operated emergency cover for the Humber ferry service for three years, .not everyone was happy with the service provided. In April 1980 the vessels owners were disappointed to hear criticism of the vessel as "not fit" by some Humberside County Councillors at a County transportation sub-committee. One Councillor told the Bridlington Free Press:

> "I, among others, felt it was hardly a suitable craft for the purpose. There was no heating, no suitable cabin accommodation, and no "mod cons". I went across on a rough day; it was cold and I had to stand there and back as I was unable to sit because life saving equipment was stacked on some seats."

Arthur Cook, for the owners, dismissed the criticisms as ridiculous, unfounded, and irresponsible. He added that while the *Yorkshire Belle* could take over 200 passengers as a pleasure boat, while operating as a ferry it could only take 110, and every passenger had to he provided with a lifejacket which was why some were on the seats and in the saloon. The Department of Trade and Industry had confirmed that the *Yorkshire Belle* met their very stringent standards. David Craft, assistant manager of the Humber Ferry, said.

> "As far as I can see the Yorkshire Belle is a very nice vessel. It is adequate for an emergency."

To counter the criticisms, the owners of *Yorkshire Belle* invited the local press to look round the craft which they said was "pristine". John Harrison, fleet services manager for Bogg Holdings Group, explained that in view of the criticisms the Press should see the condition of the boat which had a new bar, new cushion to make the wooden seats more comfortable and had been painted inside and out.

An unusual incident occurred in June 1980 when a man and a woman refused to disembark from the *Bridlington Queen,* they abused the skipper and police who were called to Bridlington harbour had to send for reinforcements to help remove them. When police arrived at the boat the couple still refused to leave, so ropes were bound around their waists and they were hoisted up onto the quayside. At Bridlington Magistrates Court they admitted being drunk and disorderly and were fined £25 each.

The *Yorkshire Belle* briefly changed her role in July 1980 from pleasure cruiser to rescue boat when she rescued two men from the sea after their yacht had sunk. The pleasure boat went to assist after spotting the yacht's distress flares. A wave had swamped their boat about a mile off the coast near Wilsthorpe. They fired three flares and hung onto the boat until she sank. When the *Yorkshire Belle* arrived to take them to safety they were clinging to a large wooden paddle.

1981 started with the news that negotiations were being conducted with several interested parties for the sale of the 33 year old *Bridlington Queen* and the story was confirmed on the 19th March with the news that its owner, Councillor Des Connelly, was selling it to a consortium in Dundee for trips on the River Tay. It was also revealed that two local men, Andrew Connelly, son of the owner, and Peter Wardill would go with it and operate it as captain and engineer respectively. The reason given for the sale was declining demand and the ever increasing cost of maintenance which meant that there was no longer enough business in Bridlington to support three pleasure boats. They had decided to go to Dundee because of the enthusiasm of the local council for the project to run river trips on the Tay after an absence of about 20 years. After refitting and with little ceremony, the *Bridlington Queen* left for Scotland and service on the Tay at Dundee as the *Tay Queen*. Her subsequent history is detailed in appendix 4.

11
And Then There Were Two

Flamborian and *Yorkshire Belle*

The departure of the *Bridlington Queen* meant that Bridlington was down to two pleasure boats, the *Flamborian* and *Yorkshire Belle,* for the 1981 holiday season which brought mixed weather with May being sunny but with few visitors. August proved to be holiday boom time as temperatures in Bridlington soared to 79 degrees, the hottest in the country and good weather in October brought a late boost to the holiday trade.

On the 11th February 1982 after nearly ten years of ownership, Bogg Holdings sold *Yorkshire Belle* for a five figure amount to her current owners Peter Richardson and Roy Simpson who both live in Bridlington. Peter, who worked for several years in the textile industry in Huddersfield, said:

> "I have always had a love of boats since a child and I thought this was a great opportunity to get away from the run of the mill job and do something I wanted to do."

Roy was a soft drinks salesman in Huddersfield but in 1981 worked as an engineer on the Bridlington pleasure boat *Flamborian*. Roy and Peter met in Huddersfield some years ago and at that time, made regular visits to Bridlington and heard, quite by accident, that the *Yorkshire Belle* might be coming on the market. They decided there and then that if this was true they would go ahead and buy her, It was true and they did. After preparing the vessel for Board of Trade inspection so that it could be ready to put into operation for the 1982 Easter holiday they announced plans to continue one-hour cruises to Flamborough Head and two-hour cruises to Filey Bay, costing about £1 and £2 respectively, and their intention to organise school trips and bring back evening disco and jazz cruises. One new idea that proved to be very successful was trips to Bempton seabird colony from a new vantage point onboard the *Yorkshire Belle*. About 150 people made the first trip in June, organised by Scarborough and District RSPB group, it was the first time birdwatchers had taken to the sea on this scale. The trip was conceived by Bridlington RSPB member John King as part of the RSPB's "Springtime is birdtlme" campaign and attracted bird-lovers from all over the country. It also gave the warden of the Bempton sanctuary. Gyr Penn, a chance to survey birds nesting lower down the cliffs. "We were able to get a much closer view than we would get from the cliff top," said Gyr. Also among the group was Brian Channon (group leader Scarborough and District RSPB members group), and Ian Armstrong North Eastern region officer for the RSPB who said

> "To see those enormous cliffs from sea-level was astounding, at one time people used to shoot the birds from the sea, but we were just shooting with cameras".

For the Bridlington boatmen the 1980's continued much the same as before, the day / weekend holiday makers either came in droves or not at all depending on the weather, which as always proved to be the deciding factor. There were visits by Royal Navy warships, mostly minesweepers of the Ton Class, which added interest to holidaymakers on the pleasure boats. The annual Harbour Gala in August was very popular and culminated in a firework display and *Yorkshire Belle* and *Flamborian* with brass cannons pitted against each other in mock battle. One year the winner was *Flamborian* aided by a speedboat with a mock

Exocet missile!

The pleasure boats continued to make 'special' trips including one in August 1984 when the ToC H Action Group arranged for fourteen underprivileged Irish children from Londonderry to have a trip on *Flamborian*, another *Flamborian* special was 'Operation Neptune' part of the relaunch of the Yorkshire Branch of the National Trust. Decked out in flags and bunting the *Flamborian* left Bridlington for Scarborough where a party of 180 Trust members were piped onboard by Scarborough sea cadets. *Flamborian* took the party on a four hour trip from Scarborough to Robin Hood's Bay as part of the Trust's campaign to save the coastline. These 'specials' were in addition to the usual range of cruises which are described in the advert below:

TAKE THE SAIL OF THE CENTURY
WITH BRIDLINGTON PLEASURE STEAMERS!

"YORKSHIRE BELLE"
"FLAMBORIAN"

Special two hour cruise every morning round the caves to view the famous seabird sanctuary, the high cliffs of Bempton and Speeton, and the spectacular geological fault. Also one hour trips throughout the day to Flamborough Head. All cruises feature live commentary and saloon bar. Light refreshments are available on the longer cruises. Both ships comply with the highest Dept. of Trade standards.

BUY YOUR TICKET AT THE PAYBOX ON THE NORTH PIER
AT BRIDLINGTON OR PHONE BRIDLINGTON 603081/76588/73582
FOR ADVANCE PARTY BOOKINGS

In 1986 Maritime Leisure Ltd applied to Bridlington Harbour Commissioners to berth the *Nassau*, a 101-foot-long ferry, in the harbour and operate it as a bar and bistro. Maritime Leisure Ltd operated the Flying Dutchman boats in Wakefield and York, the Regal Lady in Scarborough and similar boats in Spain. The company had been refused a berth for the *Nassau* in Scarborough Harbour and decided on Bridlington after being impressed with the new Crane Wharf redevelopment. The *Nassau* was built in 1939 and had operated on the Norwegian fjords during WW2, where she was seized by the Norwegian resistance movement and used for night raids. Bridlington Harbour Commissioners stated at the time of the berthing application

"If it could be located without detriment to those who use the harbour, we may well grant permission. But we are not overburdened with space."

Talks continued on the plan which saw several twists and turns with the *Nassau* being replaced by *Regal Lady* and then by *Swanage Queen*. Eventually the plans for a floating bar and bistro in Bridlington harbour did not materialise.

A very extensive survey of Bridlington holidaymakers during the 1986 season concluded, not unsurprisingly, that 60% of British families took their main holiday abroad and holidays at home were second holidays of three or four days duration. For the boatmen the good news was that visitors to Bridlington put the harbour at the top of the list of attractions, even higher than the beaches, with 94% saying they had visited the harbour compared with 76% who had been on the beaches.

In 1987 the RSPB hired the *Yorkshire Belle* to take passengers around Flamborough Head to the base of the cliffs on a series of 'Puffin Cruises' to give passengers a puffins' eye view of the spectacular seabird colonies. The cruises ran twice a month from April until July. The cruises lasted approximately three hours and an expert guide was on board to give a commentary and help identify the birds. The RSPB commented

> "People do not need to be experienced birdwatchers to enjoy these cruises - even if they have never watched birds before, they will soon be able to identify the comical puffin and to watch the majestic gannets as they plunge headfirst into the sea in pursuit of fish". Tickets for the trips were priced at £4 for adults and £2 for children. These trips proved so popular that they are continued to this day.

By 1987 the *Yorkshire Belle* was still basically in her original 1947 (stage 1) configuration and she needed updating and modernising to compete with *Flamborian*. The only major change had been the replacement of her Crossley diesel engines with twin Gardiner 8 cylinder 152 bhp engines in March 1951.

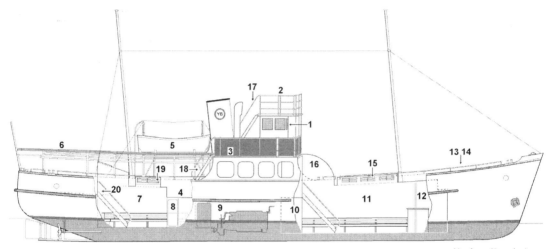

(Authors Drawing)

Yorkshire Belle before her 1987 refit (stage 1 - as built in 1947)

Covered Wheelhouse (1), Upper (Flying) Bridge (2), Bridge Deck (3),Main Deck (4), Ships Boat (5), Deck Awning and Framework (6), Ladies Cabin (7), Ladies Toilet (8). Engine Room, (9), Toilet (10), General Passenger Saloon (11), Bar (12), Sparred Seating (13), Buoyant' Seats (14), Deck Skylights (15) (for the general passenger saloon), Companionway (16) (to the general passenger saloon), Double Steps (17) (from the upper bridge to the bridge deck), Single Steps (18) (port and starboard from the bridge deck to the main deck), Deck Skylights (19) (for the Ladies Cabin), Companionway (20) (to the Ladies Cabin).

The only weather protection for passengers on deck was the canvas awning and the four cutout 'windows' were unglazed. Anyone wishing to sit down in more comfort away from the elements had to use the main passenger saloon or the ladies cabin that were located in the hull, as was the refreshment bar and toilets. Changes were also needed to meet customer expectations of what a modern pleasure cruiser should be, so during 1987 *Yorkshire Belle* underwent her first major extensive alteration at Hepworths boatyard at Paull on the Humber – the same yard that had reworked *Boys' Own* into *Flamborian*.

The canvas awning and its framework (6) were removed and the ladies saloon (7) made into a storeroom and its deck skylight (19) removed. The main passenger saloon (11) was shortened by moving the bar (12) back towards the companionway and the ladies (8) and gentlemen's toilets (9) moved from the hull onto the main deck either side of the bridge structure. The port and starboard steps (18) from the bridge deck to the main deck were doubled up on the port side by moving the starboard steps over. The superstructure was extended aft by inserting a new section (21) with three additional cut out windows each side. The aft mast (22) was stepped into the top of the extended superstructure and the wooden rescue boat (6) relocated on the extended roof. The spared seating (13) around the sides had fitted cushions where it ran through the superstructure and additional cushioned bench seating (23) with space underneath for lifejacket stowage was added under the new superstructure.

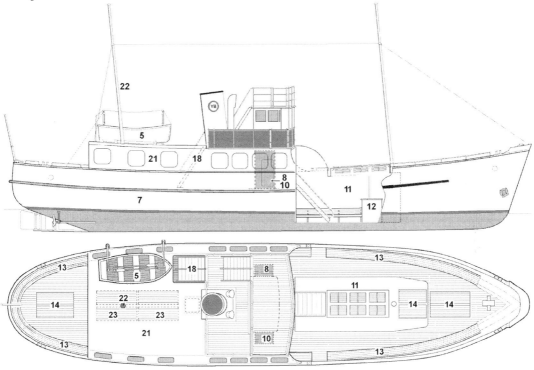

(Authors Drawing)

Yorkshire Belle after her 1987 refit (stage 2)

The newly configured *Yorkshire Belle* returned to service and together with *Flamborian* continued to cruise from Bridlington. 1988 was *Boys' Own / Flamborian* half century, 1938 – 1988 and there was a proposal to rename her *Boy's Own* again but this never came about. The early 1990's saw Bridlington host the National Off-shore Power Boat Championships which gave an added interest to events in the Bay. In July 1993 the boating fraternity was shocked by the sudden death, at home, of Desmond Connelly, owner of the *Flamborian*. Desmond (Des) was also a record breaking parachutist and a scuba diver and his son Julian was the current skipper of *Flamborian*.

An unfortunate accident marred the Harbour Gala in August during the gala's grand sea battle, when the *Yorkshire Belle* 'battled' with the *Flamborian*. The event should have culminated in a firework display but a man aboard the Yorkshire Belle sustained flash burns when the firework he was lighting ignited, blowing out two wheelhouse windows and slightly damaging the boat. Skipper Peter Richardson turned the boat back into harbour, bringing the display to a halt. The injured man, believed to be from the company that supplied the fireworks, was treated by lifeboat personnel and St. John Ambulance workers before receiving hospital treatment. The incident left the gala organisers with about £500 worth of unused fireworks. The incident also raised concerns that the event was becoming more difficult to stage because the sponsorship from local businesses would not be sufficient to cover the insurance premiums.

In 1995 further changes were made to the safety equipment on *Yorkshire Belle* as shown below.

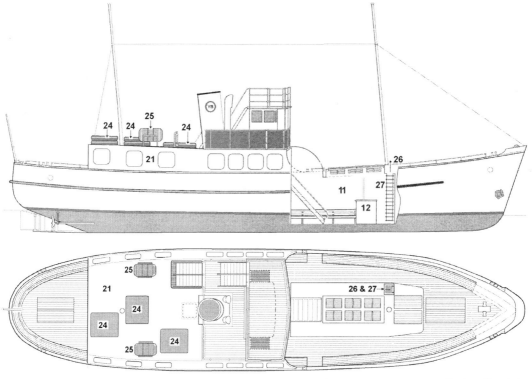

(Authors Drawing)

Yorkshire Belle after her 1995 refit (stage 3)

Some of the changes were to meet the tightened safety regulations after the loss of the *Marchioness* on the river Thames in 1989. The wooden rescue boat (6) and its associated derricks and launching gear were removed and replaced by three buoyant life rafts (24) and two modern RFD Ferryman self-inflating life rafts (25) – each capable of carrying 65 persons, were installed on the roof of the extended superstructure (21). An escape hatch (26) with a rope ladder (27) was installed on the main deck above the rear of the bar counter (12) to provide an additional escape route from the main passenger saloon (11). These additional safety improvements resulted in permission from the Board of Trade for *Yorkshire Belle* to go outside the 15-mile limit of her 'class six' licence and visit Scarborough. The last pleasure boat from Bridlington to do this was the *Thornwick* in 1965 and on Friday 7th July 1995, after a period of 30 years, *Yorkshire Belle* made a day trip to Scarborough while the *Coronia* made a reciprocal journey to Bridlington.

Tragedy struck the *Flamborian* owners again in October 1995 with the sudden death of Julian Connelly in October 1995 at the age of 40. Flags at the harbour were flown at half mast as a mark of respect, ownership of the *Flamborian* now passed on to his wife Andrea who continued to operate the vessel with the help and support of the relief skipper John Covington, local boat owners and the owners of the *Yorkshire Belle*. By this time the only major change to *Flamborian* had bee the removal of her two wooden masts which seems to have taken place sometime in the late 1980's or early 1990's.

The two Bridlington pleasure boats continued to make their 'special' trips and nearly 100 ornithologists on a *Yorkshire Belle* seabird cruise in September 1996 got more than they bargained for when a 70ft whale, surfaced beside them. The stunned bird-lovers were nearly six miles off Flamborough Head when a huge fin whale began circling the boat and diving beneath it. Bird watcher Roger Gibson from Bridlington said

> "Everybody forgot completely about the birds when the whale appeared; we were all enthralled."

The mammoth mammal stayed with the boat for over an hour, diving beneath it and easily matching its pace. Although basking sharks had been spotted, a whale had never been seen before, it seemed undisturbed by the boat and passed as close as 150 yards to it as it fed and when it breathed water spout squirted two metres into the air. Needless to say the *Yorkshire Belle* was late back in the harbour that evening but passengers and crew alike said

> "to heck with the birds, stay with the whale."

For the second year running the German cruise liner *Vistamar* visited Bridlington in 1997, the 14,000 ton cruise liner dropped anchor in the bay. The pleasure boats *Flamborian* and *Yorkshire Belle* found useful trade in transporting more than 250 passengers from the ship to the shore, coaches took some passengers to York while others stayed in Bridlington. *Flamborian* and *Yorkshire Belle* also provided trips in the bay to view the *Vistamar*.

At the end of the 1997 summer season, Andrea Connelly reluctantly decided to put *Flamborian* up for sale and the pleasure boat was effectively laid up in Bridlington Harbour. Nearly nine months later, on Thursday June 18th 1998, it was revealed that the *Flamborian* had been sold and was to leave Bridlington on Tuesday 23rd June. She was Bridlington's oldest pleasure boat and for 60 years had taken hundreds of thousands of holidaymakers on trips along Bridlington's beautiful coastline. However before she left she was to run a special day of trips from the harbour on Sunday 21st June giving her many fans the chance to say a fond farewell as she had not sailed commercially at all in 1998. The weather was glorious on Sunday 21st June as the *Flamborian* made three nostalgic final trips carrying Bridlington passengers for the last time with Roy Simpson, joint owner and skipper of the *Yorkshire Belle*, in command. Many people had come to say farewell and recalled fond memories of the *Flamborian* and when it was the *Boy's Own*. Mrs. C. A. Armes from Sheffield had very happy memories of *Boy's Own* when the skipper was George Johnson and his son's little Scottie dog named Whisky had a little coat with the name *Boy's Own* on it like the rest of the crew. Retired gardener Jim Gunningham and his wife Betty from Leeds said:

> "What more wonderful way to see the coast than sitting on the deck of a ship like the *Flamborian* and being taken out to sea - it is a sad day for Bridlington."

These thoughts were echoed by former owner Andrea Connelly who said:

> "The *Flamborian* is part of Bridlington's history and a lot of people are very fond of her - she'll be sadly missed."

Trevor Silverwood who owned her as *Boys' Own* and converted her into *Flamborian* added

> "A piece of Bridlington's history will vanish when she sails over the horizon."

On Tuesday 23rd June 1998 *Flamborian* sailed out of Bridlington Harbour for the last time on her way to her new owners, Croson Ltd and the Bournemouth Pool and Swanage Steam Packet Company (the same Company that had purchased the *Thornwick* from Bridlington in 1965 and transformed her into the *Swanage Queen* before selling her in 1970.) Her new owners planned to rename *Flamborian* as *Swanage Queen* and sail her from a restored Victorian pier at Swanage, on a daily service between Pool Quay and Brownsea Island. The subsequent history of *Flamborian* is detailed in appendix 4.

(Authors Collection)

Flamborian departing on a trip from Bridlington Harbour

12
The Last Bridlington Pleasure Boat

The *Yorkshire Belle*

On Wednesday 24th June 1998 Bridlington was down to one pleasure steamer from the eight it had in 1938 and it was left to the *Yorkshire Belle* to carry on the proud tradition of pleasure trips from Bridlington Harbour.

The importance of time, tide and weather were reinforced in 2001 when *Yorkshire Belle* got 'stuck' in Bridlington Harbour, she had set sail on Tuesday morning 20th August 2001 at 11.15am for a three and a half hour cruise to Filey Bay and back. Within an hour of leaving Bridlington fog set in and Skipper Peter Richardson decided to turn for home on safety grounds. Unfortunately *Yorkshire Belle* was caught by the ebbing tide as she reached her moorings by the north pier and as Peter explained

> "We were only feet from the harbour wall but too far away to get passengers off, typically by then the fog had cleared."

Around 50 of the 100 adults and children on board were able to be taken ashore by the harbour speedboats until they too were unable to move due to the receding water, the rest opted to stay aboard until the tide rose at 3pm some two and three quarter hours later, Peter added

> "We had offered to put a ladder down so people could walk off but we had no takers,"

So on their cruise to nowhere, passengers enjoyed the sunshine, the view, the attention, and free tea or coffee and of course the bar was still open.

In May 2002 The East Coast's biggest floating birthday party took to the waves to celebrate 55 years of pleasure cruising by the *Yorkshire Belle*. More than 60 invited guests, among them hotelier's, guest house owners, local businessmen, and members of Bridlington Town Council set sail on a birthday cruise around Flamborough Head to North Landing and back. It had been hoped to get to Bempton but the seas were a bit too choppy. On board were the Mayor and Mayoress of Bridlington, Councillor Norman Hall, MBE, and his wife Zena.

Yorkshire Belle underwent two further modifications to her superstructure in 2000 and 2002. The first modification came at the end of her 2000 season when the view from the interior of the superstructure was improved by enlarging the three 'window' sections (28) each side at the rear. Ventilation in summer was also improved by fitting the new enlarged 'windows' with removable glazed panels. The second modification to the extended superstructure was more extensive and completely changed the means of access to the main deck and the interior of the superstructure. The double steps (18) on the port side leading down from the top of the superstructure to the main deck and interior were removed and the hole in the superstructure plated over. One set of steps (29) was re-installed at the rear of the superstructure and attached to a small extension (30) to the roof structure. The blank side panel between the window on the original short superstructure and the window on the extended section was made into another window (31) making eight windows each side including the three large 'window' sections (28) that were added in 2000.

Access to the main deck and the internal areas was now from the flying bridge (2), down the port side steps (17) to the bridge deck (3), along a new walkway (32) on the top of the extended superstructure (21) to the small extension (30) and down the rear steps (29). Guard rails (33) were added each side of the new walkway (32).

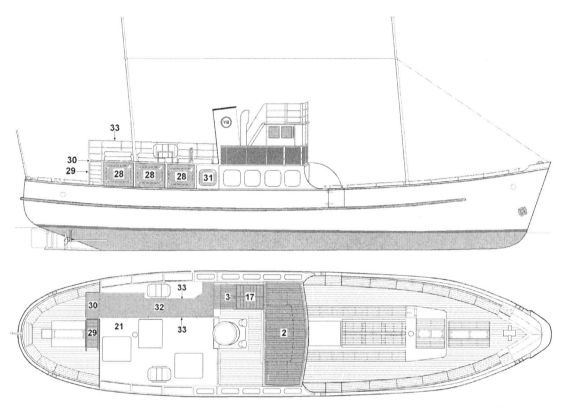

(Authors Drawing)

Yorkshire Belle after her 2000 / 2002 refits (stage 4)

With the increasing emphasis on safety The *Yorkshire Belle* and the RAF rescue helicopter regularly practice emergency procedures together and in 2005 they had to do it for real when a pensioner had to be air-lifted from the pleasure boat after suffering a suspected stroke. The pleasure boat was north of Flamborough Head when an 80-year-old woman from Doncaster was taken ill and drifted in and out of consciousness. The *Yorkshire Belle* called Humber Coastguard requesting an ambulance to wait at Bridlington Harbour but the Coastguard decided the best way to get the casualty medical treatment was to call the helicopter from Leconfield which picked her up and took her to Scarborough Hospital. Skipper Peter Richardson commented that it was something they had practiced many times but this was the first time in his 24 years at the helm that the crew had to do it as a real emergency.

The *Yorkshire Belle's* annual 'special' cruises to Scarborough were day return trips and they were matched by day return trips to Bridlington by the *Coronia*. In 2006 *Yorkshire Belle's* trips from Bridlington were scheduled weekly on Fridays in June, July and August and *Coronia's* trips started weekly on Thursdays from Scarborough. Co-Incidentally Scarborough's *Coronia,* the second vessel to bear the name, was built at Great Yarmouth as

Brit (2) to replace the original *Brit* that had moved to Bridlington and became *Princess Marina.* Yorkshire Belle's day return trips to Scarborough were alternate morning and afternoon departures from Bridlington with Skipper Peter Richardson's commentary on Flamborough Head, Bempton Cliffs and the passing coastline being given on the way to Scarborough. Arrival or departure at Scarborough can coincide with a low tide in which case *Yorkshire Belle, Coronia* and *Regal Lady* have to wait in the bay and take turns to disembark or embark their passengers at the harbour.

(Authors photograph)

Yorkshire Belle in Bridlington Bay - September 2005

In May 2007 *Yorkshire Belle* celebrated her 60th birthday (Diamond Anniversary 1947-2007) and to commemorate the event Bridlington Mayor Councillor Raymond Allerston and Consort Christine Allerston presented the owners and skippers, Peter Richardson and Roy Simpson, with a coat of arms wall plaque and a framed citation which now hang in the *Yorkshire Belle's* saloon bar. *Yorkshire Belle* set sail from Bridlington harbour for a celebration trip with a passenger list of civic dignitaries and other individuals from the *Yorkshire Belle's* past including previous crew members, *a* former skipper and some regular patrons. There were also representatives from the Harbour Commissioners including the Harbour Master and Chief Executive. Members of Bridlington Town Council and some previous Mayors of Bridlington were also on board. Two very fine models of the *Yorkshire Belle,* made by members of the Bridlington Model Boat Society, were also on display, one model depicted *Yorkshire Belle* as she appeared in 1947 and the other model showed her as she appeared in 2007.

The *Yorkshire Belle's* 2007 trip to Scarborough was particularly well attended as many people felt that this might be the last opportunity they would get as these trips came under threat with the news that 'new EU rules' would ban them in 2008. The initial reports had concerned the *Coronia* at Scarborough but would also affect the *Yorkshire Belle* at Bridlington and were related to interpretation of the 15 mile clause. Later clarification in a press release by Yorkshire and Humber MEP Richard Corbett on the 31 August 2007 revealed that it was British maritime regulations, not EU regulations that are the problem for *Yorkshire Belle* and *Coronia*. The press release explained:

> "When the *MV Coronia* was prevented from making its traditional voyage, it was reported in the media that these restrictions came from Brussels. I have since found out that these restrictions have been put in place not by the EU, but by our own Maritime Coastguard Agency. In fact, should the Maritime Coastguard Agency simply apply the EU Directive, the *MV Coronia* would indeed be allowed to make the voyage from Scarborough to Whitby with no restrictions. Under the EU Directive, the *MV Coronia* would be allowed to sail up to 15 miles from the <u>nearest harbour,</u> but under the British law, the *MV Coronia* is not allowed to sail more than 15 miles from <u>its point of origin</u>."

However the situation was not quite as simple as a re-interpretation, or misinterpretation, of the 15 mile clause. EU Directive 98/18/EC on maritime safety was introduced in 1999 based on British proposals to improve the safety of its own and other domestic passenger fleets across Europe, the directive also equated the British classification of vessels to the EU classification of vessels. UK classes II (A) to VI (A) were reclassified as EU classes A to D and *Yorkshire Belle* and *Coronia* became Class C vessels and under the EU directive could sail up to 15 miles from the <u>nearest harbour</u> which they did from 1999 to 2007. The MCA however claimed they had always interpreted the rule as 15 miles from <u>the point of origin</u> but was fairly lenient in applying it. However in 2007 the MCA decided to apply its UK interpretation to the new EU classes and it is this restriction which prevents *Yorkshire Belle* and *Coronia* from sailing more than 15 miles <u>from their point of origin</u>. After 2007 *Coronia* would be unable to sail the 17 nautical miles to Whitby and *Yorkshire Belle* would be unable to sail the 21 nautical miles to Scarborough. Ironically *Yorkshire Belle* could go to Filey (about 15 nm) but would have to come straight back as there is nowhere to land in Filey, this would take three hours compared with the two hours it takes to get from Bridlington to Scarborough.

On Friday 7th September 2007 the *Yorkshire Belle* left Bridlington on what may prove to be her last trip to Scarborough, civic dignitaries from Bridlington watched her depart and Scarborough civic dignitaries welcomed her on arrival. The impending ban was uppermost in people's minds and many people had taken the day off, cancelled meetings, altered schedules and travelled long distances just to be there.

Last tickets to Scarborough?

(Authors photograph)

The end of an era?
Yorkshire Belle, Coronia and *Regal Lady* at Scarborough – 7th. September 2007

So after 15 years of safely operating day trips to Scarborough the *Yorkshire Belle* left Scarborough to return to Bridlington with the very real possibility that if the ruling was not sorted out, Friday's trip would be their last.

In 2008 *Yorkshire Belle* operated cruises between April and October, safely and without incident. By the end of her season in 2008 and despite protests, petitions and the efforts of MEP Richard Corbett, the MCA have not altered its UK restrictions to the EU directive and *Yorkshire Belle,* operating in accordance with MCA restrictions, did not run any day trips to Scarborough and *Coronia* did not run to Whitby or to Bridlington.

Despite this setback *Yorkshire Belle's* popularity remains undiminished. A recent article in the Times newspaper by Journalist Chris Haslam, who spent six weeks travelling 4,666 miles around Britain's coastline in a campervan and then picked his best experiences from his journey, named the *Yorkshire Belle* as Britain's best boat ride.

At the end of her 2008 season *Yorkshire Belle* was sailed to Rix Petroleum boatyard at Paull on the Humber for her annual inspection, only minor work was required and she sailed back to Bridlington in January 2009 to carry out her program of cruises between April and October. These include daily one-hour cruises along the Heritage Coast to Flamborough Head and longer scenic cruises around Flamborough Head to view the dramatic Yorkshire Coastline with views of the cliffs, caves, geological faults and the RSPB Bempton Bird Sanctuary. There are also evening and ghost cruises in the bay and RSPB guided cruises to Bempton but the crises to Scarborough are still banned.

Occasionally there is something extra to see as happened on 23 July 2009 when passengers on an evening disco cruise were treated to the sight of dozens of dolphins swimming alongside the boat. They were later confirmed as White Beak Dolphins and it was only the fourth time in about 20 years that they have been seen off Bridlington.

In August *Yorkshire Belle* rescued two exhausted men who had been carried out to see on an inflatable by strong winds. The men were picked up and landed ashore at Bridlington

Harbour. *Yorkshire Belle's* 2009 season ended on the 31 October with an evening 'Ghost Cruise' which was most appropriate as it was Halloween night.

The *Yorkshire Belle* in 2010

In 2010 *Yorkshire Belle* will be 63 years old but she is very different from the boat built in 1947. Her original engines have been replaced. The single safety boat has been replaced by two modern self inflating life rafts plus three modern buoyant life rafts. The original short 'open' superstructure has been substantially lengthened to provide much more covered space for her passengers. Further improvements have been made by closing off the forward and aft ends of the superstructure with access doors and adding glazing panels to the 'windows'. Radar and up to date navigational aids have also been installed. Whilst these changes have to some extent compromised her classic appearance, they have provided the extra benefit of greater weather protection and safety for her passengers.

Safety regulations over the years have also varied the number of passengers that pleasure boats can carry and *Yorkshire Belle* is no exception. Originally licensed to carry 207 passengers in 1947, capacity was increased to 212 by 1982 when purchased by Peter Richardson and Roy Simpson, this was quickly reduced to 210 as the 212 figure was a miscalculation by the authorities and following the tragic loss of the riverboat *Marchioness* on the Thames in 1989 this was further reduced to 206.

The *Yorkshire Belle still* embarks and disembarks passengers from the North Pier via a purpose built mobile gangway onto the vessels flying bridge. Tickets can be purchased from the pay booth at the town end of the pier which also has details of the various cruise itineraries available. Groups are also catered for and the vessel is available for private charter and party bookings.

To maintain compliance with her licence, and be fully capable of meeting the latest safety and operating regulations, the *Yorkshire Belle* is sailed to Rix Petroleum (formerly Hepworths) boatyard at Paull on the Humber for her annual inspection. This is done in the winter months, between November and March, which is her closed season. This boatyard has been responsible for the refits and upgrades to the pleasure boat since 1947. After inspection and any remedial work have been completed the *Yorkshire Belle* is sailed back to Bridlington to carry out her program of cruises between April and October.

13
The Sailing Cobles, Motor Cobles and Angling Boats

When Bridlington developed as a Holiday Resort in the late 1800's there were many people who did not want the longer trips made by the larger paddle steamers and were content with a trip in Bridlington Bay in one of the many traditional sailing cobles that plied from the North Pier, the Crane Wharf Jetty or the Broad Steps. The coble is thought to date back to the Viking ships and is characterized by its wooden 'clinker' built hull, sharply raked stern, twin bilge keels (or drafts), a long rudder going deep beneath the hull, a jib sail on the bowsprit and a large 'lug' sail on the mainmast. Cobles could be found from Spurn Point to Berwick-on-Tweed and most were built locally. In 1902 Bridlington had over 80 cobles sailing from the harbour, these cobles were multi purpose, being used to take provisions out to ships in the Bay, commercial fishing in winter and taking parties of holidaymakers for a sail in summer.

(Authors Collection)

Three Sailing Cobles Leaving Bridlington Harbour c 1913
Left is *Blue Jacket* and right is *Albatross*

After the early 1900's coble numbers declined due in part to the coming of the steam trawler that made inshore fishing by sailing cobles uneconomical. The loss of fishing revenue was partially offset by the ongoing development of Bridlington as a holiday resort and a rise in the number of people using the cobles for pleasure or angling trips.

After WW1, Government aid enabled owners to convert sailing cobles to engine power, the main mast was usually retained and the sails were stowed away. All this was not done quickly and many coble owners stayed with sail power into the early 1920's or waited until their coble was ready to be replaced with a new 'motor coble'.

By the mid 1930's the sailing cobles at Bridlington had all been fitted with engines, initially petrol engines of about 9.5 hp had been used but these soon gave way to diesel engines of 16 – 24 hp. As the engines developed and became more reliable motor cobles, both old and new, dispensed completely with the sailing rig allowing a relatively uncluttered deck area. The 'new build' motor cobles were a much more versatile boat, could venture further out and were used for commercial fishing rather than pleasure trips. The arrival in Bridlington of large motor boats like *May Morn* and *Britannia* plus dedicated pleasure boats like *Princess Marina* and *Royal Jubilee* meant that the cobles were no longer the first choice for pleasure trips.

The loss of pleasure trade to the larger boats was partially offset by the increasing popularity of pleasure angling and on the 14 April 1923 the first of a series of sea angling competitions was held at Bridlington by the newly formed Bridlington Sea Angling Association (BSAA). The first event attracted 51 "ladies and gentlemen" in the five cobles *Lily, Kate & Violet, Two Sisters, Liberty,* and *Vera Mary,* with a steward on each boat. Further events were held monthly and the Bridlington Business Men's Association (BBMA) also began to organise fishing competitions, their second event in June attracting fourteen motor and sailing cobles. More competitions were held in July and August and the success of these first events prompted the BBMA to organise a Sea Angling Festival in September under the auspices of the Mayor, Mayoress, the Corporation of Bridlington and Rear Admiral and Lady Gaunt. No fewer than 11 cups and trophies plus other prizes to the value of £250 were offered for competition. Prizes also went to the skippers of the motor and sailing cobles which had on board the competitors with the heaviest catches. The motor coble winner was the *Three Brothers* skippered by B. Crawford and the sailing coble winner was *Rose* skippered by F. Shaw. The following cobles are known to have taken part, *Lily, Kate & Violet, Two Sisters, Vera Mary, Margaret, Arrow, Albatross, Mayflower, Young Tom, Florence, Rose, Three Brothers, Ocean Bride Kathleen, Rosamund,* and *Sunflower.* The competition was not limited to cobles and the motor boat *Oojah* also took competitors to sea.

Two more competitions were held in September and October and the final event of the year was a Sea Angling Tournament organised by the Star of Hope Lodge of the Royal Antediluvian Order of Buffaloes (RAOB). Now well established, sea angling went from strength to strength, providing much needed revenue for the coble owners. Apart from the war years, angling parties and competitions also increased in popularity. In September 1949 the by now annual Bridlington Sea Angling festival ran from Monday to Thursday and attracted over 500 competitors each day, so many that the pleasure boat *Britannia* was used to get 52 anglers out to sea, the other eighteen cobles taking part being full. At the end of an angling trip or competition many a Bridlington landlady would be presented with the 'catch' to be cooked, for in those days it was the custom for the visitor to provide the food to be prepared by the landlady as part of his board.

The number of anglers peaked at the 1949 level and then tapered off throughout the 1950's and 1960's, by the middle of the 1960's there was an average of about 350 in the competition and around ten angling cobles. The angling cobles could not survive on competition angling alone and many skippers had regular angling customers all year round. This led to open conflict in the 1967 competition when three of the cobles failed to turn up, preferring to take their regular anglers on a days fishing and leaving fifty competition anglers stranded without a boat to take them out.

During the 1960's motor cobles began to appear with covered wheelhouses and hydraulic steering, making life much more comfortable for the crew. These modern motor cobles were mainly used for commercial fishing as surprisingly most of the cobles used for angling parties and competitions were still those in use from the 1900's.

(Bridlington Library)

Angling Motor Cobles in Bridlington Harbour c 1968

The large coble on the left, in the picture above, is *Kathleen* and the coble on the far right is *Lily,* both these cobles took part in the first series of angling competitions held in 1923. The competition events were not limited to angling boats and it was not unusual to see the resident speedboats *Blue Bird* and *Swift* plus the larger motor boat *Britannia* taking anglers on board.

By 1971 the Bridlington angling festivals were averaging about 250 competitors per day, representing a requirement for some twenty plus angling boats. In addition to this were the scores of angling parties from clubs and institutions locally and further afield in addition to individual anglers who came as holiday makers. Competition numbers started to decline during the early 1970's to an average of around 175, however this initially seemed to have little impact on the number of angling boats, some of which were also fishing or potting commercially as well. By 1975 there were still twenty seven 'pleasure fishing cobles' at Bridlington with a total licensed capacity of 724 passengers as shown in the Table on the next page.

Angling competition numbers continued to decline and in the 1978 competition only eight boats were required; the poor weather also played a major part in this event. Although sea angling is an all year round activity and generally a safe sport, the North Sea could still spring some surprises in winter and in this competition seven anglers and the skipper were saved from the coble *'Silver Line'* that was swamped in a force 8 gale off Flamborough Head. The other seven angling boats in the group returned safely. The 1980 competition was even worse with only six boats needed for the competitors who only numbered between 93 -110 per event. Amongst the six boats used was Neil Newby's new angling boat *King Fisher.* Angling numbers picked up but the weather could still throw a spanner in the works as in the 1983 fishing contest when 24 angling boats carrying 350 anglers were permitted to sail from the harbour in a force 10 storm. An angler became ill on *'Sea Jay'* and the angling boats were escorted to safety by the Bridlington lifeboat. Not to be deterred, the angling boats went out the next day and *'North Wind'* and *'Royal Endeavor'* got into difficulty.

Pleasure / Fishing Cobles at Bridlington in 1975

Boat	Owner / No of passengers		Boat	Owner / No of passengers	
Britannia	M. Tranmer	55	*Primrose*	H. Champlin	30
Frances	L. Broadbent	36	*Young Tom*	L. Jenkinson	30
Kate and Violet	L. Jenkinson	36	*Yorkshire Lass*	J. Brooks	28
Kathleen	P. Firth and A. Jenkinson	36	*Comrade*	C. Harrison	12
			Dorothy		12
Liberty	H. Champlin	36	*Edith*	W. Harrison	12
Lily	A. Newby	36	*Emmanuel*	D. Brown	12
White Heather		36			
Monica	E. R. Newby	36	*My Judith*	S. Dodgson	12
Our Freda	C. Wright	36	*Nancy*	H. Smith	12
Rosamond	H. Champlin	36	*North Wind*	P. Cockerill	12
Rose	G. Broadbent	36	*Silver Line*	C. Emmerson	12
Three Brothers	N. Newby	36	*Sunflower*	E. Train	12
Speedwell	S. Dodgson	35	*Two Sisters*	M. Jenkinson	12
Mermaid	C. Harrison	30			

By the mid 1980's more modern boats in wood, steel and later GRP had began to appear with modern diesel engines, wheelhouses, electronic navigation and fish finding equipment. There were now thirty boats in Bridlington's angling fleet comprised a mix of older cobles and more modern boats like *Aqua-Star, Sportsman* and *King Fisher.* Traditional coble building was a declining art and one of the last wooden motor cobles was *Emma Jane,* built by Tony Goodall at Whitby in 1987 for Bridlington Skipper Tony Screaton, she was used for commercial fishing not angling.

By the latter part of the 1990's, the older cobles built for sail and then converted to motor cobles and used for angling, were long gone. All the later motor cobles had also left the angling fleet, some being used for commercial fishing or potting, the rest broken up or sold for private use, their names sometimes being perpetuated by a modern replacement. One sailing coble that still exists at Bridlington is the *'Three Brothers'.* Built by local boatbuilders Baker and Percy Siddall in 1912, she was fitted with an engine after WW1. In 1984 she was purchased by Bridlington Harbour Commissioners and converted back to a sailing coble. *Three Brothers'* is currently sailed and maintained by the Bridlington Sailing Coble Preservation Society (BSCPS).

At the start of the new millennium the number of angling boats in Bridlington had declined to about a dozen modern and far more capable fast launches catering for anglers either in parties or as individuals. The angling boat numbers have stabilized at around this figure although it is not unusual for some of the boats to stop angling and take up commercial fishing / potting provided they have the appropriate licenses to do either or both. All angling boats are fully licensed to operate 3, 6, and 8 hour angling trips, tackle and bait can be provided if required and the vessels have electronic fish finder aids, VHF radio, radar and carry approved Department of Transport life-saving equipment. They leave Bridlington harbour at various times dependent on tide and weather conditions and usually operate off Flamborough Head.

(Authors Photographs)

An old coble name is perpetuated by the modern wooden angling launch *Liberty*

The wooden angling launch *Heidi J* with an angling party off Flamborough Head

The Bridlington Sea Angling Festival is currently a Sea Angling Week that is held in early September with full day and half day fishing competitions. There are 16 cups, 9 trophies, 2 shields, 1 rose bowl and cash prizes for the heaviest fish caught. The angling fleet vessels operating between 2005 and 2009 are listed in the following Table.

The Bridlington Angling Fleet between 2005 and 2009

Name	Reg No.	Anglers	Description
Amaka Rose	H467	12	Wooden angling launch built in 1978. Carvel built hull.
Heidi J	H544	12	38 ft. wooden angling launch built in 1980. Clinker built hull.
Kimberley	H131	12	GRP angling launch built in 1989.
Liberty	SH287	12 - 36	40 ft. wooden angling launch. Clinker built hull. Single screw.
My Girl Gill	---	12	GRP angling launch.
Ocean Crusader	---	12	40 ft. GRP angling launch built in 1989. Twin screw.
Providence	H144	12	GRP angling catamaran.
Rachel K	---	Up to 40	Wooden angling launch. Clinker built hull. Single screw.
Striker	---	12	Lochin 33 GRP angling launch.
Tri-Star	H395	12	GRP angling launch built in 1990.
Yorkshire Lass	SH235	12	10 metre GRP angling launch built c1982. 120 bhp Perkins diesel engine driving twin screws.
Yorkshireman	---	12	Wooden angling launch. Carvel built hull. Single screw

14
The Powerboats

One of the earliest references to speedboats at Bridlington is in May 1929 when a new speedboat licensed by the Corporation arrived from Grimsby and

> "was a great source of interest as it sped along the edge of the bay at over 40 mph."

Not everyone however was enamored with the idea of the speedboat particularly the fishermen and they made an official objection. After making their objection it was suggested that if they were worried about loss of trade why did they not club together and buy a speedboat of their own, they then applied for a license to ply for hire with a 10 seater speedboat. This led to the Town Council receiving a petition against speedboats signed by the fishermen, some of whom were at the same time applying for a license to operate a speedboat. The petition was unsuccessful but a consortium of eight fishermen was granted a license. In July 1929 complaints were received on 'high speeds' when entering and leaving the harbour and that 'more discretion and a little more clothing' should be encouraged among the passengers. The problem of high speed led to the Clerk to the Harbour Commissioners issuing a final warning to the owners that speedboats must not be driven at more the 3 mph within the harbour limits (which included the water within 150 yards (137.2m) of the seaward side of the piers).

In July 1930 it was reported that the Harbour Master had refused to allow 'hydrophone' (sic) speed boats to operate from the harbour – whether he meant 'anymore speedboats' or wanted to get rid of those already operating is not stated. By this time at least four speedboats, *Thriller, Nippy, Rose Marie* and *Speedy* were operating at Bridlington. *Speedy,* owned by J Spencer, *was* lost in August 1931 when the petrol driven speedboat burst into flames as her tarpaulin cover was removed to make her ready for the afternoon trade. The burning boat was quickly towed out of the harbour by the motor coble *Primrose* and beached on the sand where she burnt herself out, leaving her owner with an estimated loss of £1000.

The speedboats carried thousands of holidaymakers safely across the bay in the summer season but in August 1933 there was a serious accident when two of them, *Rose Marie* and *Nippy* collided in the harbour entrance. The bow of *Nippy* drove into the side of *Rose Marie* and rescue boats rushed to the scene to take passengers off the speedboats that were now 'locked' together.

(Bridlington Library)

Rose Marie in Bridlington Harbour

Two injured men were taken to the Harbour Master's house where the Harbour Master's wife 'rendered first aid and gave the injured men restoratives'. They were subsequently taken to hospital where stitches were inserted in the cuts and the men discharged. Some of the other passengers were only slightly injured but all suffered badly from shock. The *Rose Marie* soon filled with water and sank near the South Pier.

In October 1936 a new 27 foot (8.2m) long, 250hp speedboat arrived by rail. Her owner James Newby had paid £1200 for her and she (name unrecorded) had upholstered armchair type seating for 12 passengers. In March 1937 she was joined by the speedboat *Sweetheart* which arrived from America to be operated by Tom and Herbert Hutchinson. *Sweetheart* was built by Chris-Craft of Algonac, Michigan who were one of the first mass producers of powerboats. Powered by a 160 hp engine she could make 45 mph and was soon in the news when in April 1937 she rescued 3 men in three rowing boats. One rowing boat had capsized, the second had broken an oar and the 3 men were in the third boat attempting to row back to the harbour against a strong wind and tide. *Sweetheart* took the 3 men onboard while a second speedboat towed in the rowing boats.

(Arthur Newby)

Sweetheart in Bridlington Bay

Tom and Herbert Hutchinson subsequently sold *Sweetheart* to Walter and Neil Newby and they operated her until war was declared on the 3rd September 1939 and all pleasure boat activity, including speedboat rides, ceased.

The fate of the speedboats at Bridlington during WW2 is unknown and it is unlikely that any pre-war boats were serviceable when the war ended in Europe in May 1945. By August the Bridlington Piers and Harbour Commissioners announced that they had received several applications for speedboat licenses, no doubt influenced by the availability of cheap ex-naval craft after WW2, though many were worn out and did not last very long, neither did their engines!. However the Commissioners agreed with their Works Committee that considered them a danger to small craft and other users of the harbour and decided that no speedboats would be allowed to ply for hire from the harbour or any place over which the Commissioners had jurisdiction. At that time the issue was academic as the military authorities did not declare the harbour safe until May 1946. It is unclear how long the speedboat ban lasted but by the early 1950's Bridlington had at least four speedboats, namely *Speed, Sweetheart, Blue Bird* and *Swift* running trips into Bridlington Bay. *Blue Bird* and *Swift* arrived in 1951 and were two ex-RAF high speed launches powered by twin Perkins engines driving twin screws, the Jenkinson family owned *Blue Bird* with G. Jewitt as skipper and 'Don' Connelly owned *Swift* with D Freeman as skipper. In addition to speedboat rides *Blue Bird* and *Swift* sometimes took anglers to sea in the angling competitions. *Sweetheart* operated until 1954 when she was sold away and replaced by *Skylark*.

(Arthur Newby)

Skylark in Bridlington Bay with Neil Newby at the controls

By 1959 there were four permanent berths for speedboats in the harbour and over the next 30 years various speedboats came and went as due to the arduous nature of their work speedboats have a relatively short life. Their high performance engines last for about five or six seasons and their hulls rarely last beyond ten. The speedboat *007*, owned by P. Jenkinson, arrived in 1963. It was not unusual for her to be used to investigate reports of wayward rubber dinghy's, etc. In the summer of 1965 she rescued seven people in difficulties off Wilsthorpe, four were from a broken down motor boat drifting out to sea and the other three were people who had attempted to swim out and get the drifting boat ashore, the boat was subsequently towed in by *007*.

(Bridlington Library)

007 in Bridlington Harbour c1968

In June 1967 *007* rescued two people from a dingy that had blown over in strong winds. Initially *007* had a blue hull with *007* in black lettering and a polished wooden deck; she was probably refitted after 1968 as she was reported later with a red hull and *007* in white lettering. *007* operated from the 1960's until the early 1970's, which was a long time for that type of speedboat.

In the 1970's *007* was joined, or replaced, by *U2* and *Splashdown,* both speedboats being owned by Paul Jenkinson. These speedboats of the 1970s were powered by inboard engines but their propellers were mounted on outriggers. Their drive shafts passed through special couplings that enabled the propellers to be twisted so that steering was achieved by re-directing the propeller rather than using a conventional rudder.

The 1980 speedboats included *Hi-jack* and *Thunderbird, Hi-jack* owned by the Jenkinson's found herself in trouble with the authorities in 1983 when complaints were received that she had approached too close to the beach on her high speed runs and was endangering swimmers in the water.

In 1992 Neil Newby introduced a competitor for the Jenkinson's speedboats in the shape of his new (unnamed?) red and white 27 foot (8.3m) high performance powerboat from Ring Powercraft Ltd.

By the early 1990's the powerboats operating from Bridlington were Neil Newby's Ring 27 powerboat and the Jenkinson's *Terminator.*

(Arthur Newby)

Neil Newby's Ring 27 powerboat

Terminator was taking passengers on a ride in Bridlington bay in August 1993 when they heard an 'almighty bang' and the boat started to sink. Skipper Ian Rollisson ordered passengers to don lifejackets and fired a distress flare as two nearby fishing boats raced to the rescue and lifted passengers to safely, with any children being taken off first. Boat owner Paul Jenkinson was on shore when the accident happened, but immediately jumped into a boat to go and help. He said the rescue 'went like clockwork' and none of the 12 passengers on board got their feet wet. The *Terminator* remained submerged for almost seven months after it sank, the stern half of the speedboat eventually washed up on the south side of the harbour, behind the Spa, in late February 1994 and the bow half was found at Sewerby Steps and had to be dragged up the side of the cliff before it could be taken for storage. The boat's engine however had not been located and former owner Paul Jenkinson, said he was not involved in the recovery of the *Terminator* and the boat was now the responsibility of his insurance company in London.

Between 1993 and 1994 the remaining Bridlington power boats were joined by *Enterprise* and in 1994 *Shockwave* arrived for owner Bob Pickering. *Shockwave* was a new 'state of the art' 27 foot (8.3m) high performance powerboat, the hull of which was built by Mike Rigg of Ring Powercraft Ltd at Littlehampton. All the fittings and the 350hp turbocharged Sabre Marine diesel engines and Italian manufactured jet units were fitted at Bob's engineering works in Scarborough. The 350hp turbocharged engines gave *Shockwave* a top speed of 39 knots.

The appeal of the new powerboat was overwhelming and after eight weeks of competition Neil Newby sold his Ring 27 powerboat to Bob Pickering, who stripped off the old decking, leaving the hull and engines. New seats and a new top deck produced a new running mate for *Shockwave* in the form of *Mirage* which was introduced into service in 1995.

(Authors Photograph)

Shockwave in Bridlington Bay in 2005

After 10 and 14 years respectively of arduous service '*Shockwave*' and '*Mirage*' were replaced in early 2006 by two new powerboats *Purla* and *Sonic*. This time Bob had the new boats built to his requirements by Hunton Powerboats at Ramsey in Hampshire, a specialist builder of high performance, hand crafted powerboats. *Purla* and *Sonic* are based on a shortened 34 foot (10.3m) version of the 37 foot (11m) long Hunton RS/XRS 37 design which can trace its performance lineage to the 1990 Guernsey gold cup winning hull. *Purla* arrived in Bridlington in April 2006 and ran alongside *Shockwave* until *Sonic* joined her in late May. *Shockwave* was then sold away to Ilfracombe and *Mirage* is currently operating from Scarborough as *Rocket*.

Both *Purla* and *Sonic* are fitted with twin Volvo 350hp D6 marine diesels and capable of a top speed of 52 knots, some 13 knots faster than their predecessors. They are licensed to carry 12 passengers each on high speed trips in Bridlington Bay, but pregnant women, people with backache and those of a nervous disposition are advised not to participate.

These ultra modern powerboats have water-jet drive units that use an impellor to produce a high speed jet of water at the stern, steering and reverse drive are achieved using baffles that re-direct the jet in the appropriate direction

(Authors Photograph)

Purla in Bridlington Bay in 2006

Approximate service dates for Bridlington speedboats and powerboats

Date	Speedboat(s)
1930's	*Thriller, Nippy, Rose Marie* and *Speedy*
1936	*Sweetheart* and one other
1950's	*Speed, Sweetheart, Blue Bird* and *Swift*
1960's	*007* and *U2*
1970's	*Splashdown*
1980's	*Hi-jack* and *Thunderbird*
1990 - 1994	*Terminator, Enterprise* and unnamed Ring 27
1994 - 2006	*Shockwave* and *Mirage*
2006 - current	*Purla* and *Sonic*

15
The Theme Boats

Theme Boats are a recent addition to the harbour scene at Bridlington and were first introduced towards the end of the 1990's when Bridlington fishermen and boatmen, along with their counterparts in the rest of the UK, faced declining fish stocks and were forced to diversify to make ends meet. The Newby families, who have been connected with the sea for more than 200 years, decided to convert their 1979 built angling boat *Sportsman* into a tourist 'Theme Boat'. *Sportsman* was given two tall masts, yards, furled sails, flags, bowsprit and poop deck, renamed the *Pirate Ship* and repainted as a galleon. In May 2000 owner Sean Newby, son of Arthur Newby the youngest of the three Newby brothers, hoisted the skull and crossbones and set sail towards the old smugglers' caves under Flamborough Head with his first party of tourists.

The *Pirate Ship* is based in Bridlington all year and operates whenever the weather permits and passengers are waiting, embarking and disembarking up to 53 passengers (12 in winter) from the steps on the Chicken Run jetty for a sail ride in the Bay. The route is

varied so there is something new to see and weather permitting the *Pirate Ship* will go up to Flamborough Head. Tickets can be purchased from the pay booth at the start of the jetty; this is unmistakable as it is 'guarded' by a large statue of a pirate complete with eye patch. A pirate flag can be purchased and judging by the number of children clutching their flags she is a very popular boat.

(Authors Photograph)
The *Pirate Ship* in Bridlington Bay

In 2002 a second theme boat appeared with the arrival of *Shark Attack*, a theme conversion from the wooden angling launch *Sea Jay*, built in 1984 at South Shields. Slightly smaller than the *Pirate Ship* she had a dummy shark on her wheelhouse roof, a fake hole painted on her hull and she could accommodate up to 52 passengers (12 in winter) for trips in Bridlington Bay. In 2004 *Shark Attack* was sold to the Newby family and renamed *Jaws*. The dummy shark remained on the roof but the fake hole on the hull was replaced

(Authors Photograph)
Shark Attack in *Bridlington Bay in* 2004

by shark's teeth either side of the bows. Jaws operated up to November 2006 when it was announced that she was up for sale due to the retirement of her skipper, Arthur Newby.

At the end of 2007 the dummy shark on the roof was removed, the boat repainted as a conventional passenger carrying launch and was sold away to North Wales in November 2008.

In 2004 local fisherman Tony Pockley launched "What's in the Pot?" experience trips on his new angling catamaran *Providence*. This entailed taking people on a 30 minute trip into Bridlington Bay to haul various shell fish pots and explain what was in them and how they were baited and operated. However this innovative project resulted in a re-classification of *Providence* as a theme boat with a substantial increase in its license fee which, the boat owner believes, makes the idea uneconomical. With the "What's in the Pot?" experience trips in abeyance *Providence* is currently operating as an angling / potting / workboat, licensed to carry 12 passengers.

(Authors Photograph)

Providence on a "What's in the Pot?" trip in 2004

By the start of the 2009 season, *Providence* was no longer operating "What's in the Pot?" experience trips and *Shark Attack / Jaws* had been sold away. The Bridlington theme boat scene has now gone full circle with only the *Pirate Ship* operating as a 'Theme Boat', the very same boat which started the trend in the late 1990's

Appendix 1

Timelines for the Paddle Steamers at Bridlington

The table below shows the timelines for the paddle steamers known to have been frequent visitors to Bridlington. At the height of the paddle steamer activity at Scarborough there were many other paddle steamers that were running pleasure trips along the East Coast. These paddle steamers included *Eclat, Contraste, Fame, Sir Colin Campbell, Minnet, Xantho, Superb, Lady Londesborough, Avalon, Emu* and *Camperdown*, none of which are thought to have been regular visitors. The Yarmouth registered *Comet* of 1876 was seen at Bridlington in the 1890's but this was thought to be an isolated occasion.

Name	Years at Bridlington
Transit	1852-1853
Confidence	1853-1855
Friends	1874 only
Forth	1900 only
Cambria	1900-1912
Scarborough	1866-1914
Frenchman	1899-1927
Bilsdale	1925-1934

1914-1918 war

Appendix 2
Listing of the Paddle Steamers known to be regular visitors at Bridlington

PS *Transit*
Type	Wooden sloop rigged paddle tug		
Tonnage	14 tons (burthen)	*Length* 65.6 feet (20 metres)	
Builder	Unknown, Built in 1848 at Shields for service at Leith.		
History			

Re-registered in 1852 at Scarborough under the ownership of Jeremiah Hudson. Based at Scarborough and running pleasure trips to East Coast resorts including Bridlington. Sold in 1854 and re-registered at Sunderland.

Ultimate fate - unknown, replaced at Scarborough by the PS *Éclat*.

P S *Confidence*
Type	Iron paddle steamer
Tonnage	103 tons (gross) *Length* unrecorded
Builder	Built in 1862 at Jacksons Yard Middlesbrough for the Royal Mail Steamboat Co.
History	

Operated passenger services Middlesbrough-Whitby-Scarborough, also trips from Scarborough to Whitby and Bridlington. In the winter she was used for towing colliers on the river Tees. Registered home port was Middlesbrough.

Ultimate fate - unknown.

P S *Friends*
Type	Iron paddle tug
Tonnage	75 tons (gross) *Length* unrecorded
Builder	Unknown, Built in 1866 at Shields.
History	

Carried passengers during the summer months only, recorded as working out of Bridlington at various times. Registered home port was Shields.

Ultimate fate - unknown.

P S *Forth*
Type	Iron paddle steamer
Tonnage	144 tons (gross) *Length* unrecorded
Builder	Unknown, Built in 1883 at Shields.
History	

In 1900 *Forth* was used for ferrying passengers out to the coastal steamer *General Havelock*, she is known to have made several visits to Bridlington. Registered home port was Grangemouth.

Ultimate fate - unknown.

P S *Cambria*
Type	Iron paddle tug
Tonnage	174 tons (gross) *Length* unrecorded
Builder	Unknown, Built in 1879 at Preston.
History	

In 1899 Cambria was purchased by the Harbour Commissioners at Scarborough for use as a pleasure boat and tug, *Cambria* is known to have made several visits to Bridlington. Registered home port was Scarborough until 1913 when she was sold to Hull owners. Ultimate fate - unknown.

P S Scarborough

Type	Iron paddle steamer
Tonnage	142 tons (gross) *Length* 150 feet (45.75 metres)
Builder	Built in 1866 by Messrs Lewis and Co. in London for the Gainsborough United Steam Packet Company.

History

Scarborough was the largest paddle steamer based at Scarborough although her registered home port was Grimsby. She was a regular visitor to Bridlington from 1866 until 1914 when she left Scarborough for the breakers yard.

Ultimate fate – scrapped in 1914.

P S Frenchman

Type	Steel paddle tug
Tonnage	119 tons (gross) *Length* 90.3 feet (27.6 metres)
	137 tons (gross) *Length* 101.4 feet (30.6 metres)
Engines	Two J. P. Rennoldson & Son side level surface condensing engines capable of 225 indicated horse power.
Builder	Built as the *Coquet* in 1892 at South Shields by J. P. Rennoldson & Son for H. Andrews of Newcastle.

History

Coquet was sold to T. Gray and Co. of Hull in 1899, renamed *Frenchman* and used as a paddle tug in winter and for excursion work from Bridlington in summer. Excluding the war years *Frenchman* sailed out of Bridlington from 1899 until her final season in 1927. In 1928 *Frenchman* was working on the Humber but was taken out of service in 1929. In later years her superstructure and engines were removed and the hull used as a dumb barge by United Towing at Church Lane on the river Hull until the early 1960's.

Ultimate fate – towed to New Holland for scrap about 1963 and finally broken up in 1968.

P S Bilsdale

Type	Steel paddle steamer
Tonnage	199 / 235 tons (gross) *Length* 200 feet (61 metres)
Engines	A non-compound double diagonal engine.
Builder	Built as the paddle steamer *Lord Roberts* at Preston in 1900 by W. Allsup & Sons for the Great Yarmouth Steam Tug Co. Ltd.

History

In 1914-18 *Lord Roberts* saw war service as the *Earl Roberts* and on decommissioning in 1919 was sold to the Furness Shipbuilding Co for use at their shipyard. She was sold again in 1925 to the Crosthwaite Steamship Co. of Middlesbrough and renamed *Bilsdale*. As *Bilsdale* she was used for excursion work from Scarborough in the summer months and is known to have made occasional visits to Bridlington. Her registered home port was Middlesbrough and in September 1934 she made her last pleasure cruise out of Scarborough before she was sold for scrap.

Ultimate fate – sold for breaking up in 1934

Appendix 3

Timelines for the Screw Driven Pleasure Boats at Bridlington

Name	Years at Bridlington			
Girls Own	1922 - 1938			
Britannia	1923 - 1939	1946 1979	Later years as an angling launch	
May Morn	1925 - 1939			
Yorkshireman	1928 1939	1947 1955		
Princess Marina	1935 1939			
Royal Jubilee	1935 1938			
New Royal Sovereign	1936 1939	Sunk 1940		
Miss Mercury	1938 1939?			
Boys' Own	1938 1939	1946-1968	Became Flamborian	
Yorkshire Belle (1)	1938 1939	Sunk 1941		
Titlark		1946 only		
Bridlington Queen		1947 1980		
Yorkshire Belle (2)		1947 to date		
Thornwick		1948 1965		
Flamborian (ex Boys' Own)		1968 - 1998		

1939-1945 war

Appendix 4

Listing of the Screw Driven Pleasure Boats at Bridlington

Girls Own

Type	Passenger Carrying Motor Boat
Tonnage	10? *Length* unrecorded but probably 60 feet (18.3m)
Engines	Unknown
Builder	Unknown, believed built at Southend-on-Sea in 1922
History	

Girls Own operated from Bridlington as a licensed passenger carrying motor boat from 1922 until 1938 when she was replaced by *Boys' Own*. After *Boys' Own* arrived *Girls Own* seems to have disappeared.

Ultimate fate – unknown, possibly sold or broken up in 1938.

Britannia

Type	Passenger Carrying Motor Boat
Tonnage	10 *Length* 52 feet (15.86m)
Engines	Unknown
Builder	Hayward and Croxan of Southend-on-Sea in 1923
History	

Britannia operated from Bridlington as a licensed passenger carrying motor boat from 1923 until the late 1960's when she ceased working as a pleasure boat but stayed in Bridlington as a licensed angling boat. Over the years *Britannia* had various refits that substantially altered her appearance, she also had several owners, the last Bridlington owners being Oscar Topham followed by Mick Tranmer who sold *Britannia* to Tom Furey of Ireland in 1979 when she left Bridlington.

Tom Furey operated *Britannia* from 1979 until he sold her to Kay McDonagh in 1989.

Kay McDonagh operated *Britannia* in Ireland from 1979 until he sold her to Michael McDonnell in 1999.

Current Status - *Britannia* is currently owned by Michael McDonnell and is being operated by Viking Tours of Athlone, Ireland as a 'Viking' theme boat on the River Shannon & Lough Ree.

May Morn

Type	Passenger Carrying Motor Boat
Tonnage	10? *Length* unrecorded but probably 60 feet (18.3m)
Engines	Unknown
Builder	Unknown, arrived in Bridlington in 1925.
History	

May Morn operated from Bridlington as a licensed passenger carrying motor boat from 1925 until the start of World War 2 in 1939 when she seems to have disappeared.

Ultimate fate – unknown, possibly sold or broken up in 1939.

Yorkshireman

Type	Tug-Cruiser
Tonnage	251 *Length* 120 feet (36.6m)
Engines	Two Earle's reciprocating triple expansion engines, with direct acting vertical cylinders of 800 indicated horse power which gave her a top speed of 11.2 knots.

Builder   Earle's Shipbuilding & Engineering Company Limited in 1928 for the United Towing Company of Hull.

History

Operated from Bridlington as a licensed passenger carrying pleasure Tug-Cruiser from 1928 until 1955 when she had her last summer season at Bridlington and left to work full time as a jetty tug in the Humber. One of her saddest duties as a Humber tug was in November 1960 when the ashes of T. C. Spinks, the managing director of United Towing, were scattered at sea off Spurn Point from the deck of *Yorkshireman*.

By the early 1960's United Towing was again modernising its fleet and a few of the steam tugs were converted to diesel power but the majority were sold or scrapped. With some sadness, the decision was taken to scrap the *Yorkshireman* in 1965, by which time she was one of the last steam powered tugs in the company's service.

Ultimate fate - in August 1965 *Yorkshireman* was towed by sister tug *Workman* to Boom; near Antwerp, in Belgium, where she was broken up.

Princess Marina

Type   Coastal and River Boat

Tonnage   Unknown   *Length* over 60 feet (18m)

Engines   Two Kelvin petrol-paraffin engines

Builder   Fellows and Co Ltd. of Yarmouth in1928 as *Brit* for owners E. W. & S. H. D. Longfield

History

From 1928 *Brit* ran cruises from Britannia Pier and Hall Quay Yarmouth and from other South Coast resorts until she was sold to Albert Butler of Leeds in 1935 for service at Bridlington as *Princess Marina*. She operated from Bridlington from 1935 until June 1948 when she was sold to Sea Cruises (Whitby) Ltd and was put into service at Whitby.

In 1952 she was sold to Thorne Launches of Twickenham and served the next eight years on the Thames operating from the site of the Festival of Britain adjoining County Hall. She was owned by Alfred Crouch of London from 1960 until 1976 when Crouch's fleet was sold to George Wheeler Launches who operated from Westminster Pier on the Victoria Embankment in London.

Her history between 1976 and 1984 is not clear, when sold to George Wheeler the original intention was to withdraw her from service, however she was not withdrawn being eventually sold to the F. & B. Boat Co. of Kingston on Thames. Two years later in 1987 *Princess Marina* was sold to R. J. Turk & Sons of Kingston who sold her on to Thames Rivercruise of Caversham, Reading in 1989.

Between 1989 and 1991 Thames Rivercruise carried out a major refit of *Princess Marina* designed to bring her up to their high standards. A large amount of steel hull plating was replaced and she gained a single enclosed deck with an open fore deck and a rich mahogany interior. Inside she has a dance floor, a full galley, bar, toilets and passenger area. She was re-engined with two Ford 2700 six-cylinder diesels producing 90 hp. and an 8
kilowatt Onan generator. Radio and telephone communications equipment have also been installed together with a central heating system powered by two Webasto water heaters.

After her refit *Princess Marina* re-entered service with Thames Rivercruise of Caversham, Reading, albeit in a much modified and updated form, and was licensed to carry parties of

(Thames Rivercruise)

Princess Marina on the Thames near Gatehampton in 2005

20 to 50 people. There is a fully fitted galley with a gas hob and oven and a fully stocked bar supplying draft beers and lager. *Princess Marina* can accommodate 36 passengers for sit down restaurant meals and up to 50 people for buffet. During 2006 *Princess Marina* had a large amount of steel hull plating replaced from amidships to the bow and afterwards ran regularly as a cruising restaurant.

Current Status – in service with Thames Rivercruise as a cruising restaurant on the Thames.

Royal Jubilee

Type	Passenger Pleasure Boat
Tonnage	60 *Length* 74 feet (22.5m)
Engines	Twin Bergius built three-cylinder Kelvin K3 diesel engines developing 132 horsepower and driving twin screws
Builder	CWG Beverley in 1935 for Crawford and Pockley of Bridlington
History	

Royal Jubilee operated from Bridlington from 1935 until 1938 when she was sold to the St. Mawes Steam Tug and Passenger Co. Ltd in Falmouth Cornwall. Her new owners renamed her *New Roseland* and she replaced their fifty year old vessel *Roseland*. The *New Roseland* was used as the Falmouth to St. Mawes ferry until she was requisitioned for war service as a barrage balloon vessel in the Bristol Channel. After the war *New Roseland* returned to service at Falmouth with the St. Mawes Steam Tug and Passenger Co. Ltd until December 1967 when the ferry company was taken over by the consortium of the Smith Bros. During her time with the St. Mawes Steam Tug and Passenger Co. Ltd, *New Roseland* had her weather awning and stern mounted safety boat removed, her wheelhouse enclosed and her K3 engines replaced with a pair of Lister engines.

In April 1968, only four months after the takeover by the Smith consortium, all four ferryboats in the fleet were put up for auction but did not reach their reserve price and were not sold. The Smith Bros. eventually sold the business to a M. Miller and in 1970

New Roseland was sold to Coakley's Launches for service on the Thames. About 1979 Coakley's Launches were taken over by Tower Pier Launches, a new consortium of Thames River Craft and Woods River Cruises. New vessels entered service in 1982 / 1983 and Coakley's obsolete fleet were sold off. After her sale *New Roseland* had a colourful, but rather vague, history. She is believed to have operated on the south coast, the Clyde and in the Cromarty Firth, where she served as the Cromarty to Nigg ferry. Between 1986 and 1989 she ran pleasure cruises in the Bristol area, taking the name *Avon Venturer*. She was sold again in 1989, to a company at Newcastle upon Tyne.

Ultimate fate - In 1995 *Avon Venturer* was reported as laid up or out of service and her history from that point is unknown.

New Royal Sovereign

Type	Passenger Pleasure Boat
Tonnage	68 *Length* (reported) 81 feet (24.8m)
Engines	Two six-cylinder diesel / oil type engines driving twin screws and giving her a maximum speed of ten knots
Builder	Unknown, believed built in Southend in 1929.
History	

New Royal Sovereign plied for hire from Southend until 1936 when she was sold to Albert Butler of Leeds and a consortium of Bridlington fishermen who also owned the *Princess Marina*. *New Royal Sovereign* operated from Bridlington as a licensed pleasure boat from June 1936 until she was requisitioned by the Royal Navy in September 1939.

Ultimate fate - On the 23rd August 1940, *New Royal Sovereign* was blown up in a bombing raid on Bridlington Harbour. No crew was on board at the time.

Miss Mercury

Type	Passenger Pleasure Boat
Tonnage	Unknown *Length* 60 feet (18.2m)
Engines	Twin six cylinder Parsons engines each developing 125hp giving a cruising speed of 16 knots
Builder	Unknown, built for the Thames Taxi Service, date of build also unknown.
History	

Miss Mercury was sold to the Albert Butler consortium, who already owned New Royal Sovereign and Princess Marina, in 1938 for service at Bridlington as a licensed pleasure boat carrying up to 100 passengers. After arriving in Bridlington *Miss Mercury* started pleasure trips during the 1938 Easter holiday bur little else is known after that.

Ultimate fate – her history after her arrival in 1938 is unrecorded.

Boys' Own

Type	Passenger Pleasure Boat
Tonnage	52 *Length* 69 feet (21m)
Engines	Twin Bergius built Kelvin K4 diesel engines developing 176 horsepower to give a speed of 10 knots at 750rpm.
Builder	Built by CWG Beverley in *1938* for John, Jim and Walter Newby.
History	

Boys' Own operated from Bridlington from 1938 until she was requisitioned by the Royal Navy in 1939 for harbour duties as a boom defence vessel. In April 1940 she was sold / transferred to the Army and subsequently saw service with the Royal Army Service Corps (R.A.S.C.) on the River Tees, Tyne and Humber. *Boys' Own* returned to Bridlington in

1946 and started pleasure cruising duties once again. In 1960 *Boys' Own* was sold to Trevor Silverwood of Flamborough who had her modernised at .Hepworths shipyard at Paull on the river Humber in 1968. After modernisation *Boys' Own* was renamed *Flamborian* and returned to service at Bridlington.

Boys' Own history is continued under *Flamborian*.

Flamborian (Ex Boys Own)

Type	Passenger Pleasure Boat	
Tonnage	*unchanged at* 52?	*Length* 69 feet (21m)
Engines	Twin Gardner 6LXs rated at 116hp.	
Builder	Built by CWG Beverley in *1938 as Boys' Own*	
History		

Flamborian operated at Bridlington from 1968 until 1998 when she was sold to Croson Ltd and the Bournemouth Pool and Swanage Steam Packet Company (trading as the Dorset Belles), who planned to rename her *Swanage Queen* and operate a daily service between Pool Quay, Swanage and Brownsea Island. On Tuesday 23rd June 1998 *Flamborian* left Bridlington to take up her new duties at Swanage in Dorset. However, the plan to change her name to *Swanage Queen* was dropped and she continued to operate as *Flamborian* on cruises along the Dorset coast. These cruises ceased when the operators and the harbour authorities could no longer agree for *Flamborian* to operate from a key site within the harbour. After a refit she was put up for sale in Devon. In 2004 she was sold to Stuart Line Cruises of Exmouth in Devon who planned to have her cruising again on the River Exe and along the coast between Exmouth & Sidmouth by 2006. Unfortunately these plans also could not be achieved because the work that would have been required to meet the latest regulations was more extensive than had been anticipated. Effectively, this meant that it would not be feasible for any operator to restore *Flamborian* for passenger service.

Current Status – in April 2005 Frenchman Phillipe Kermoal purchased *Flamborian* for conversion into a cruising yacht, mobile office and houseboat at Villennes-sur-Seine some 30km from Paris. He has plans to convert her in a manner that is sympathetic to her character and design.

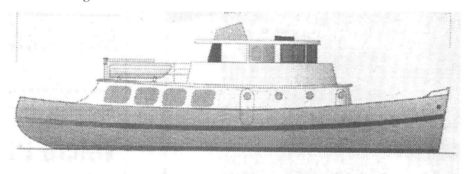

Flamborian conversion *as* planned by Phillipe Kermoal

Yorkshire Belle (1)

Type	Passenger Pleasure Boat
Tonnage	56 *Length 76 feet (23.2m)*
Engines	Twin Bergius built Kelvin K4 diesel engines developing 176 horsepower to give a speed of 10 knots at 750rpm.
Builder	CWG Beverley in 1938 for Crawford and Pockley of Bridlington
History	

Yorkshire Belle operated from Bridlington from 1938 until she was requisitioned by the Royal Navy on the 23 November 1939 and used for patrol duties and as a boom defence vessel.

Ultimate fate - Yorkshire Belle sank with all hands on 11th April 1941 after an underwater explosion (believed to be caused by a magnetic mine) 3½ cables (640m) from Haile Sand Fort in the river Humber.

Titlark

Type	Passenger Pleasure Boat
Tonnage	details unknown *Length 70 feet (21.35m)*
Engines	Parson's petrol/paraffin engines driving twin screws.
Builder	Jake Bolson and Son of Bournemouth (Skylark Shipyard) in 1936
History	

Titlark 1 and her sister *Titlark 2* operated cruises from Bournemouth for Jake Bolson and Son. *Titlark 1* was sold to Holiday Camp Cruises Ltd. and operated at Bridlington for one season only in 1946. During 1946 she was sold to Dawson, Newman & Westall and may have operated out of Scarborough in 1947, but with no evidence to support this and in view of the hostility to her there, this is thought unlikely and her immediate whereabouts after she left Bridlington are unknown. In 1952 she went to County Cruises of London along with her sister *Titlark 2* and on the 8th June 1957 both boats passed to Thames Launches of Twickenham, *Titlark 1* was renamed *Okra and Titlark 2* was renamed Oleander. The service history for Okra after 1957 is unrecorded.

Ultimate fate - Titlark 1 registration was closed on 19th July 1965 and her history after that is unknown.

Bridlington Queen

Type	Passenger Pleasure Boat
Tonnage	22.95 *Length 62 feet 10 inches (19.2m)*
Engines	Twin Dorman engines, later replaced by twin 88 hp Lister Blackstones.
Builder	Adapted from a MFV by Watercraft Ltd., East Molesey, Surry in 1947 for R Ingram of Sheffield who also owned Britannia.
History	

Bridlington Queen operated at Bridlington from 1947 until the end of the 1980 season when she was sold away to Dundee. She saw service at Dundee on the Tay as the *Tay Queen* and then at Boscombe before being laid up at Southampton. Further service followed at Newcastle-upon-Tyne, running cruises in the late 1980s and early 1990s. For some of this time, she would be running alongside the former Bridlington cruiser *Royal Jubilee*. She also featured as the setting for an episode of a popular religious programme that was broadcast on national television. Shortly after this Chris Eborall took her to Nottingham where about £8000 was spent on her. The work included a modern wheelhouse, located on the main deck rather than on the flying bridge (presumably done to allow passage under low bridges) and an engine overhaul. After this she sailed several times from Nottingham Trent Bridge to Gunthorpe Lock but eventually ended up languishing in Cromwell Lock. By 1995 she was in a very poor condition and several items, including her builder's plate had been removed, possibly by vandals. One report claims that she was then towed to Goole where local company Viking Civil Engineering Ltd. were given the task of breaking her up. However it now seems that Alan Oliver of Doncaster undertook the sad task of removing the *Bridlington Queen* from the river at Cromwell lock and subsequently breaking her up. Alan had agreed to salvage the '*Queen*', intending to restore her for his own use as a cruiser and/or restaurant, but she was too badly damaged for this purpose and proved to be too small for use as a restaurant. During her breaking up Alan found that she had different gearing on the two engines – 3:1 reduction on one and 4:1 on the other!

Ultimate fate – Broken up by Alan Oliver of Doncaster in 1995.

Thornwick

Type	Passenger Pleasure Boat
Tonnage	126 *Length* 100 feet (30.7m)
Engines	Twin Gardner 8L43 engines, each of which developed 150 hp. at 900 revolutions
Builder	D. E. Scarr Ltd. of Howdendyke in 1948 for Albert Butler of Leeds.
History	

Thornwick operated at Bridlington from 1948 until 1965 when she was sold Croson Ltd. and the Bournemouth, Swanage and Poole Steam Packet Company to replace their paddle steamer Embassy. *Thornwick* was extensively refitted, one of her two funnels was removed and her bridge was enclosed. In 1968 she operated trips from Bournemouth to Totland Bay and Yarmouth in the Isle of Wight but at only 10/11 knots she proved too slow for the Isle of Wight runs and Croson acquired the 12 knot *Coronia* from Scarborough. The fleet was renamed with *Coronia* and *Thornwick* becoming the *Bournemouth Queen* and *Swanage Queen respectively*. As *Swanage Queen* she was used on ferry runs from Bournemouth to Swanage Pier but was eventually withdrawn at the end of the 1969 season and sold to Meridian Line Cruises of Greenwich on the Thames in December 1970. Between 1971 and 1984 she was often moored near the naval college and the National Maritime Museum and ran charters from Greenwich and Westminster, her Official Number was 181336 and she was licensed to travel as far as Southend. At this stage she was fitted with additional covered rear accommodation, giving her a very unbalanced appearance. In 1980 she was registered at Pool, 127gt, 86nt, and owned by Joan V John and Edward T Barnard of Kent. In the 1990s she was sold and became a houseboat on the River Medway, her name reverted to *Thornwick*, but further modifications to her superstructure make her look like a very unattractive blue and white floating tram. Her engines have been removed and it is most unlikely that she will ever sail again.

Current Status – for sale in 2007 as a three deck house boat on the River Medway, quite unrecognizable as the attractive Bridlington pleasure steamer she once was.

Yorkshire Belle (2)

Type	Passenger Pleasure Boat
Tonnage	30 *Length* 80 feet (24.4m)
Engines	Twin Crossley 8WM6 diesel engines, each developing 120 bhp to give a top speed of 10.3 knots.
Builder	Built by CWG Beverley in 1947 for Bride Hall Pockley of Bridlington
History	

The second *Yorkshire Belle* has been cruising at Bridlington from 1947 to date. Over the years Yorkshire Belle has had several major changes made to her to maintain compliance with the latest safety and operating regulations. During her long career *Yorkshire Belle* has had several changes of ownership. In September 1969 ownership passed from Bride Hall Pockley to John Cross Pockley and Thomas Marshall Neeham of Bridlington. Four years later in 1973 she changed hands again and became the property of J. T. Bogg, Arthur Strike Cook and J. F. Bogg, all of Bridlington and operating as Bogg Holdings. She stayed in their ownership for nearly ten years until she was sold again in February 1982 to her current owners Peter G. Richardson and Roy Simpson of Bridlington.

Current Status – *Yorkshire Belle* is in service at Bridlington with owners Peter G. Richardson and Roy Simpson as a pleasure steamer licensed for 206 passengers. In May 2007 she completed 60 years of service.

(Authors photograph)

Yorkshire Belle entering Bridlington Harbour in 2008